# FIFTY YEARS IN THE CLASSROOM
and What I Learned There

A Memoir

By John Barsby

◆ FriesenPress

One Printers Way
Altona, MB R0G 0B0
Canada

www.friesenpress.com

**Copyright © 2022 by John Barsby**
First Edition — 2022

All rights reserved.

No part of this publication may be reproduced in any form, or by any means, electronic or mechanical, including photocopying, recording, or any information browsing, storage, or retrieval system, without permission in writing from FriesenPress.

Cover photo of the Grade Ten classroom in the Dominion City school was taken by the author in 1965

ISBN
978-1-03-915071-3 (Hardcover)
978-1-03-915070-6 (Paperback)
978-1-03-915072-0 (eBook)

1. BIOGRAPHY & AUTOBIOGRAPHY, EDUCATORS

Distributed to the trade by The Ingram Book Company

# Table of Contents

Introduction .................................................... vii

Chapter I.
*The First Day* .................................................... 9

Chapter II.
*A New School – A New Province* .................... 17

Chapter III.
*Middle School Years* ...................................... 23

Chapter IV.
*High School* .................................................... 31

Chapter V.
*The Knock On The Door – Teaching At Age 19* ...... 39

Chapter VI.
*Snow Lake, Gordon Bell, St. John's-Ravenscourt* ...... 47

Chapter VII.
*The Experimental Years At Gordon Bell* .......... 59

Chapter VIII.
*Teaching Streamed Classes* ............................ 63

Chapter IX.
*Magic In The Classroom* ................................ 71

Chapter X.
*Observations And Opinions On Assorted Topics* ...... 77

Chapter XI.
*How It Used To Be – A Look Into Schools Of The Past* ...... 119

Chapter XII.
*The Qualities Of A Good Teacher Circa 1897* . . . . . . 153

Afterword . . . . . . . . . . . . . . . . . . . . . . . . . . . . 159

Acknowledgements . . . . . . . . . . . . . . . . . . . . . 161

# Introduction

Last night I dreamt that I was back in the classroom. It was opening day and I was handing out textbooks. It felt good to be there. Like most of my teaching dreams, this one was quite pleasant but there are also anxiety dreams. In one that occurs from time to time, the bell has rung. Classes should all be underway but I am desperately going up and down long hallways looking for my classroom and I cannot find it. It simply is not there. I expect that dream to be with me for the rest of my days. It has almost – but not quite – replaced the student anxiety dream where I am required to write an examination for a course I did not even take.

It is not surprising that in my dreams I find myself in a classroom, as a teacher or a student. Most of my life has been spent in and around schools. Fifty-three years elapsed between the day I started Grade One at the age of not-quite-six and the day I retired from teaching in June of 2004. That retirement was only partial: I did occasional substitute teaching for several more years.

The urge has come upon me to record some of my memories and observations. My purpose in writing this memoir is threefold. First, I want to paint a picture of how things used to be in the schools of my childhood and early years of teaching. The schools then, especially those in rural areas, were very different than the schools of today. In that sense, this is a historic record. Secondly, I want to share some of the insights – dare I say wisdom? – that I

### John Barsby

acquired in my decades of teaching. Most classroom teachers will find something of interest here. They may disagree with some of my opinions and, in others, find confirmation of their own. My third purpose is to entertain. This memoir can be viewed as a collection of stories. Some, I hope, will be interesting and even amusing.

These recollections take the form of a series of essays. Some deal with a particular theme. Others are anchored to a time and place. The order is chronological at first but becomes more random later on. Personal experiences feature strongly, leading to much autobiographical content. But in the midst of personal stories, I tend to wander off on tangents, discussing some educational issue or other on which I have a strong opinion. Classroom anecdotes and examples are more likely to come from the mathematics room than, say, the geography room but they should be applicable to the teaching of just about any subject. Specific references to regulations and curriculum are Manitoba based but similar to those found elsewhere.

In describing the experiences of my own student days, I identify many people by name. Later on, when dealing with the schools where I spent most of my teaching career, I am very sparing in the use of names. I do name a few administrators and colleagues who played important roles in the narrative. I do not mention any students by name. There were many great colleagues and fine students from whom I learned a great deal. If I tried to include them all, the list would be endless.

I start this memoir with my very first day of school. Let me set the stage. The year is 1951. I am almost six years old. I don't really want to go to school but it seems I do not have a choice. Turn the page and read on ….

John Barsby<br>
March 2022

# Chapter I.
## *The First Day*

The first day of each school year is always an exciting one. To me, it was always the beginning of the year, and still feels that way even in my retirement. January 1$^{st}$ is just a day in the middle of winter. The true New Year's Day is the Tuesday after Labour Day. Once, when giving an opening day address at a school assembly, I told the students that today, not some time in January, was the time for making New Year's Resolutions. I even suggested a few they might consider. Top of the list was stick-with-it-ness, the term I always used for tenacity. Students have told me years later that they still remember me talking about stick-with-it-ness, something I did with just about every class I taught. Would they have remembered if I had used the word tenacity instead? Possibly. Whatever we call it, it is perhaps the trait that comes closest to guaranteeing a student success in the school system.

When I started school back in 1951, I missed out on the official opening day, and I certainly lacked any sense of tenacity. At the time, we lived in the tiny village of Tantallon, located in Saskatchewan's Qu'Appelle Valley. My family was returning from a summer holiday and arrived home three days after the beginning of term. My sister, Pat, who was in Grade Six, was given the task of taking me to school. We did not have far to go. The four-room brick school was just across the railway tracks from where we lived.

When we passed through the door, Pat spotted some friends of hers.

"Wait here by the drinking fountain," she said, and ran off to talk to them. While I stood waiting, Miss Couch, the primary teacher, saw me and ushered me into her classroom. I tried to explain that I was waiting for Pat but I did not express myself well and I am sure she did not understand. I felt as if I was being kidnapped.

Her classroom, known as Room I, was for Grades One to Three. Kindergarten did not exist. Tantallon Consolidated School District No. 948 did not spend money on luxuries.

There were eight of us in Grade One that year, four boys and four girls. I can still remember everybody's name, except for one surname which has vanished from my memory. Grade One had the row of desks by the windows. Grades Two and Three had the other rows. These were solid desks made of wood and iron, with each row bolted to a pair of long wooden runners. I spent three years in that room and remember it in great detail. There were flags on the wall (Union Jack and Red Ensign), a piano, a sand table, and a long but narrow cloakroom with two doors and coat hooks along each side. At the front of the classroom the blackboard wrapped around three sides of a chimney forming corners that Miss Couch used when she ordered misbehaving students to "go stand in a corner." Two years later, in Grade Three with a different teacher, gum chewers had to stand in one of these corners, facing the class, with their gum stuck to their noses.

As you faced the front of that room, the windows were on the left. That was true of every room in the school, and every school in the province. It was a requirement, not only in Saskatchewan but in most Canadian provinces. The regulation dated back to a time when the windows were often the only source of illumination. All students were encouraged to be right-handed, even if it did not come naturally. Windows were to be on the left so the students' hands would not cast a shadow over what they were writing.

# Fifty Years in the Classroom and What I Learned There

The room had sounds and smells of its own. The scent of dust bane – a product used when sweeping dirt from the wooden floors – hung in the air all year. The smell of hot wet woollen mittens, attached by their thumbs to the hot air registers and left to dry, was the smell of winter. The smell of spring was the scent of the lilacs on Miss Couch's desk, brought in daily by some of the girls in the class. The sounds were the creaking of wooden floors, the rustling of papers, the voice of the teacher, and the sharp staccato sound of chalk on a hard slate blackboard. The murmuring of the twenty-some students was very subdued, if heard at all.[1] Whispering – and even talking – happened occasionally but it was highly discouraged.

And, of course, that room had the two wall maps – Canada and The World – which advertised Neilson Chocolate Bars in each of the four corners. That must have been a very successful advertising campaign; most Canadians of my generation remember these maps. Schools today would not permit such flagrant product placement but in the 1950s the lure of free teaching aids was stronger than any scruples the school authorities might have had. In 1953, the year of the Coronation, every pupil in the school was given a wooden ruler advertising Coca-Cola on the front and listing all the "Rulers" of England on the back from William I to Elizabeth II.

I was woefully unprepared for school. I had very little experience when it came to interacting with other children. My speech was difficult to understand. I had not yet learned how to pronounce the letters r and j. I avoided words with these sounds as much as possible. I dreaded it when people asked me my name because it had both of the offending sounds. Sometimes I would avoid answering by saying, "I don't know."

---

1  A class photo of Room I taken that year shows Miss Couch with twenty-two students.

In today's world I would have benefitted from a kindergarten experience, and likely from some speech therapy as well. It is easy for people my age to look on the schools of the past with a sense of nostalgia, seeing a golden age that never really existed. I am not among them. I recognize that the schools of today have much more to offer.

This four-room school in Tantallon offered Grades One to Twelve. Room II was for Grades Four through Six. Room III was for Grades Seven and Eight. Room IV was the high school room. Today, when I look back on it, it is Room IV that fascinates me. In that room the principal taught Grades Nine through Twelve, personally teaching almost every subject in every grade. How did he manage to prepare lessons for over twenty courses and do his administrative work as well?[2] At the end of the school year students wrote external exams set by the Department of Education in Regina. Not surprisingly, pass rates were low. Few, if any, students went on to higher education. If anybody wanted to do so, French was frequently a roadblock. In those days, a second language was required for entering university and, most years, the school did not offer it. When my sister reached Grade Nine, French was offered in the form of some textbook grammar taught not by the principal but by the teacher from Room III.

Our family lived in Tantallon from July 1950 to November 1955. My parents made friends there and were much involved in the life of the community. My father was the organizer of Tantallon's Golden Jubilee celebrations in 1955, marking the 50th anniversary of Saskatchewan becoming a province. They would

---

[2] That situation was far from being unique. I have some Manitoba data. In the early 1960s there were over thirty-five one-room high schools in the province. Most of them closed later in that decade when the old school districts amalgamated to form large school divisions, and regional high schools were built. [From Report of the Department of Education, 1964]

have stayed much longer if the school had been better. My father in particular was determined that both of his children would one day go to university. It was clear that Tantallon did not offer the necessary prerequisites. We moved in November of 1955, the year I was in Grade Five and Pat was in Grade Ten.

During the Tantallon years we made frequent trips to Regina, usually to go to the dentist or the optometrist. We always stayed with relatives, including a cousin who was about four years older than Pat. She went to a large city school that offered a multitude of courses. She was in the commercial stream, studying typing, shorthand, and other office skills. In those days, your educational opportunities depended very much on where you lived. The disparity in educational offerings between rural and urban schools has never disappeared but it is less pronounced today than it was then.

It was a time when hundreds of one-room country schools dotted the landscape, schools where one teacher taught Grades One to Eight. I never had the experience of attending such a school. My sister did in the years before Tantallon. A lot of people remember these schools fondly as places that fostered self-reliance and resourcefulness. My sister's experience suggests that much depended on the teacher. In Manitoba, where I have lived since 1955, most of these schools closed in the early 1960s. At that time the entire education system was overhauled, with hundreds of local school districts amalgamated into larger school divisions. This was a very expensive undertaking which required the building of many new regional schools. The premier of the day was Duff Roblin, a Progressive Conservative with the emphasis on Progressive. To pay for his expensive projects (which included building the Winnipeg floodway), he introduced the Provincial Sales Tax. In today's political landscape, it would be hard to think of him as a Conservative.

But none of these educational issues meant anything to me on that September day in 1951, when I found myself in Miss Couch's room. It must have been a traumatic experience, because the day is etched into my memory with a few lapses. I must have gone home for lunch during the mid-day break but I have no recollection of that.

I do remember that we gathered around the piano where Miss Couch taught us to sing "Row, Row, Row Your Boat". What, I wondered, is a Spuda Dream? I knew about nightmares – I had had a lot of them – but Spuda Dreams were totally unfamiliar. They didn't sound all that scary. Everybody seemed happy enough as they sang "Life's a Spuda Dream." When I got home, I asked my mother what a Spuda Dream was but she didn't understand the question. It was several years later, after I learned to read, that I finally figured it out.

I also remember that on that day I made both a friend and an enemy.

The enemy was the girl who sat behind me. At one point, when Miss Couch was not looking, she poked me in the back. When I turned around, she grasped the thumb of one hand with the fingers of the other.

"Do you know what this means?" she said.

I told her that I didn't. She lowered her voice even more, looked around furtively, and said what I instinctively knew was a Very Bad Word. It was several years before I heard that word again, so innocent was that place and time.

She poked me in the back several more times that morning but I no longer remember what it was about. After a while I started to ignore her.

Near the end the end of the day we were all given a sheet of construction paper, a pair of scissors and some glue. The task was to make furniture for a doll house. I was supposed to make a chair but it turned out badly. When the time came to clean up our mess, my soon-to-be-enemy put all her scraps of construction paper under my desk instead of depositing them in the waste paper basket. I knew nothing of the code by which children live. I reported her misdeed to Miss Couch. From then on the girl made it very clear that we were sworn enemies.

The friend I made was the boy who sat in front of me. He was a year older than I was. He had been home schooled and could already do all the work for Grade One. Clearly, he should have been placed in Grade Two but the school in Tantallon did not approve of parents teaching their children[3], and made a point of placing him in the first grade. At the end of that year he moved to Elkhorn, Manitoba where he was placed in Grade Three, so he did eventually join his age cohort.[4]

Over all, the day was not a happy experience. My father took a picture of me that morning holding a satchel with my school supplies. I look very grumpy in the picture. I clearly did not want to go, and I remember not wanting to be seen with that satchel. Then as we entered the building I was abandoned by Pat and kidnapped by Miss Couch. During the day, I struggled with the tasks expected of me. I was unable to make a chair out of construction paper. I felt totally incompetent. Then the day ended with hostilities between me and the girl behind me. On my way home, I realized that I had spent a whole day at school and still did not know how to read. What had been the point of all this suffering?

---

[3] At PTA meetings the Tantallon principal asked parents not to help their children, especially with reading. This was the era of learning to read by sight, and the fear was that parents would confuse their children with phonics.

[4] We were pen pals for quite a few years after he moved away. The last contact we had was in the summer after my Grade Ten year. By then, his family had moved from Elkhorn to Winnipeg, where I spent a day visiting him. I have often wondered what happened to him in his adult life.

When I got home, I asked my parents if it was necessary to go every day. My mother told me that there would be weekends and holidays when I could stay home. My father valued education very highly, perhaps because his own educational opportunities had been limited. He explained to me that twelve years of school would be followed by four years of university. It was a daunting prospect.

# Chapter II.
## *A New School – A New Province*

We moved to Dominion City, Manitoba late in November of 1955.[5] By then I was in Grade Five. In the weeks following the move, I suddenly went from being a very mediocre student, near the bottom of the class, to being a successful student. What happened so abruptly? In adult life, after I had become a teacher, I frequently found myself trying to answer that question. I would look at poorly performing students in my classroom and wonder if they, like me, had a more successful version of themselves lurking under the surface.

The Tantallon years had passed very slowly as childhood years do. At that stage of life there is an eternity of time between one Christmas and the next. I eventually did learn to read, and became quite an enthusiastic reader but that did not lead to great success in any school subject

I often seemed not to know what was going on or what was expected. The first exam I ever wrote was in Grade Two. I felt I had done badly, so I hid my paper inside my desk instead of handing it

---

5  Dominion City, despite its grand name, was a very small village. The population at the time was said to be about 700. This included a lot of people who lived on nearby farms rather than in the town itself. Dominion City was, however, quite a bit larger than Tantallon.

in. Miss Couch gave me zero. I remember a spelling test in Grade Three where the word dictated was *liquid*. If it had been used in a sentence, I could have spelled it. But what I heard was *lick wood*, which made no sense because it was two words not one but, not knowing what else to do, I wrote it down. I remember an early introduction to fractions where we were asked to draw a picture of an orange and then draw a picture of half an orange. I drew perfect circles for both. I was told to try again but I had no idea what else to do. The half grapefruit on the breakfast table, viewed from above, was perfectly round, and an orange would be the same.

By the time we started Grade Four, there were only five of us. Two of the boys had moved away at the end of Grade One. One of the girls had been sent to the "San" in our Grade Three year. A decree had come from Regina requiring everyone in the province to have a chest x-ray. The whole town lined up at a mobile x-ray van that was parked near the post office. Her x-ray indicated tuberculosis and she was taken away. She was still in the sanatorium two years later when my family left Tantallon.

My report card at the end of Grade Four had a place for "Rank in Class." I was ranked fourth out of five. I had failed both spelling and social studies, and barely qualified for a promotion to Grade Five. The student who placed fifth, just behind me, had to repeat Grade Four.

Then, in November of my Grade Five year, we moved to a different school in a different province with a different curriculum. The school in Dominion City was twice as big as the one in Tantallon. There were nine classrooms in use, including three in a temporary building called The Annex. Putting twelve grades into nine rooms requires some grade splitting. Grade One had its own room. Grade Two and half of Grade Three shared a room. The other half of Grade Three was in with Grade Four. But Grade Five – my grade – had a room of its own.

There were twenty-five of us, perhaps the largest class in the school. But not all of us were ten years old. The school in Dominion City routinely failed students who did not pass enough exams at the end of the year. However, there was a rule that a pupil in elementary school could only spend two years in a grade. After the second year they got a "social promotion" whether they passed or failed the exams. So, some of my fellow Grade Five students were as old as sixteen, having spent two years in each grade. By the time we were in Grade Seven, there were only thirteen of us. Of the twelve who fell by the wayside, a few had moved away but most had reached the school leaving age of sixteen.[6]

Our teacher in Grade Five was Miss Jack, a woman in her mid-twenties with five or six years of teaching experience. In the story of my progress through the school system was she a villain or a hero? She moved with us into Grade Six at the end of that year, so I had her as a teacher for two years. There were times when I saw her as a villain but now, looking back on those years, I count her among the heroes.

She certainly seemed a villain to me at the beginning. On my very first day she sent a letter home with me. I have never read the actual letter though I heard my parents discuss it. She wanted to prepare them for the fact that I would very likely fail Grade Five. She informed them that it is very difficult for a student to transfer from one province to another so late in the school year. I would have to learn all the material on the Manitoba curriculum, which

---

6   The sixteen year old students usually stayed until the end of the school year. One, however, dropped out midterm on his birthday even though he was legally required to stay until June 30th. The oldest student in the class did not drop out at sixteen. She was over seventeen when she finally quit school at the end of Grade Six. She was always very pleasant and got along with all of us. The teacher made special assignments for her since she could not handle the regular work.

was very different from Saskatchewan's, particularly in science and social studies. I would be starting out three months behind the class in these subjects and, based on my Tantallon report card, not a strong student to begin with. She did not offer much hope.

Miss Jack asked one of my classmates to lend me her notes, which I was to copy into a notebook of my own. I spent my Christmas holiday copying a hundred or more pages of notes, mostly in Canadian history and science. I was supposed to copy the English literature notes as well. The school reader that was used – a book called *Wide Open Windows* – was the same as the one I had used in Saskatchewan. There we had done exercises from an accompanying workbook. My mother encouraged me to ask Miss Jack if the exercises I had already done could count as the equivalent of the note taking that her class had done. Miss Jack was doubtful about that. She said she would give me an examination to write, and if I passed it, I could be excused from copying the notes. I passed it.

In arithmetic,[7] I was slightly ahead of my new classmates. I had already learned how to add fractions which they did not do until later in the year.[8] Yet, arithmetic became my most dreaded subject because of the homework. In Tantallon we had never had homework – that was something for older students – but Miss Jack assigned arithmetic homework every day. In my memory it seems like hours each night but it was probably a lot less than that. I remember several occasions where my mother would do some

---

[7] Today the word *mathematics* is used at every grade level. In the schools of my childhood, that word was not used until Grade Seven. Until then, the course was called *arithmetic*, even though it did include a little geometry.

[8] It is interesting to note that the addition of fractions was taught in Grade Five in the 1950s. Today, in the Manitoba curriculum, it is not taught until Grade Seven.

long divisions for me so I could be finished before the nine o'clock bedtime that we rigidly observed.

Despite all of this, however, I found myself beginning to like Miss Jack. Her classes were interesting. The students all seemed to like her, even the teenagers in her class. Something in me was awakened. We had a set of exams in February that year. My rank on the report card that followed these exams was third out of twenty-five. How had I managed to improve so much in so little time? Had I done it to prove Miss Jack wrong, to show her that her lack of confidence in me was misplaced? That was my theory at the time but as the years go by I give her more and more credit for it. I suspect that the hours I spent copying notes, the studying for that English Literature exam, and all that arithmetic homework had something to do with it. She was demanding more from me than my Tantallon teachers had ever demanded. That was a very good thing. My years of teaching have convinced me that when teachers demand very little from their students that they get very little.

I often thought about looking her up and discussing it with her but that never happened. She died a few years ago at the age of eighty-five. Today I think of her as a very good teacher.

Another memory I have of Grade Five is getting the newly approved Salk vaccine for polio. The local doctor administered the vaccine. The entire class lined up, and each of us got our shot. I have no recollection of any parental permission even being required.

Grade Six, another year with Miss Jack, passed uneventfully. It was Miss Jack's last year of teaching. She became Mrs. Grier at the end of the school year and embarked on a new career – that of dairy farmer. I missed a lot of school that year with appendicitis in November and influenza in March but still managed to be one of the top students in the class. My transformation from being a weak student to being a strong student was complete.

# Chapter III.
## *Middle School Years*

Then came the richest two years of my educational life. I was in Mrs. McVicar's room for both Grade Seven and Grade Eight – the two grades shared a classroom. She was a teacher in her late forties who had stayed home when her children were young but was now back in the classroom. I consider her to be the best teacher I had in my school years.

I have often heard educators who should know better declare that early adolescence is not a time for academic learning. Schools, they say, need to concentrate on the social and emotional needs of these students. Serious learning can wait.

When I hear that – and sometimes it comes from principals and so-called educational experts – I want to stand up and shout NO! NO! NO! That suggestion is almost criminal. If teachers expect very little from their students, that is what they will get. They will be wasting what could be the most productive learning years in the lives of their students. Given the right stimulation Grades Seven and Eight can be a time when one's curiosity about the world is insatiable, when one gathers knowledge like a sponge, one's vocabulary increases by leaps and bounds, and those who are avid readers devour book after book after book.

So it was with me in those years. Everything was interesting. Science, English Literature, English Grammar, History, Geography,

Health (a subject that emphasized human anatomy), Mathematics: I loved it all. And vocabulary! I still remember the context in which I learned words like *unique, capital* (as in money), *ablutions, alacrity, dispatched*, in my Grade Seven year. Mrs. McVicar never allowed us to glide over an unfamiliar word without learning it.[9] One of our textbooks, in a section on scale drawing, showed a picture of a bird – a phoebe – drawn one-quarter of life size. She took us out of the room one by one to see which of us had looked up the pronunciation of that word. I hadn't but I have known it ever since.

It was not just the meaning of the words that fascinated me. It was their rhythm and cadence. A phrase would lodge in my mind like an earworm, and I would go through the day endlessly reciting to myself things like "the silken sad uncertain rustling of each purple curtain."[10] I had a good memory for poetry. I could quote passages from just about every poem we studied. I started writing my own poems and short stories. I still have a box filled with hundreds of pages of immature efforts from my time in Grades Seven and Eight.

And reading! I easily read three books a week, and sometimes more. I quickly exhausted our very limited classroom library. Some classmates who were also avid readers loaned me their own books in exchange for borrowing mine. Because most of them were girls, I was exposed to a heavy diet of Nancy Drew, Kay Tracey, and

---

9   My vocabulary was expanding at a rapid pace. Whenever I learned a new word, in the days that followed, I would often find it over and over again in my reading. Clearly, it had always been there, but I had glided over it without paying attention. I particularly remember learning the word *ubiquitous*. Within a week, I decided that *ubiquitous* was ubiquitous.

10  From "The Raven" by Edgar Allan Poe. It was a poem I had read on my own, not one that we studied at school. All these years later, I can still quote the opening lines.

Trixie Belden. In return, they got to read the Hardy Boys. Some of them even read the short mystery stories that I wrote myself, each consisting of eight to ten densely typewritten pages and very imitative of the series books that we were all reading.

Then I learned about The University Extension Library which would send me books through the mail and pay the return postage. They provided their customers with a catalogue but it did not mean much. Most of the time, the librarians ignored what I ordered and substituted books of their own choosing. And what choices! I was introduced to Richard Jeffries's *Bevis* which became a lifetime favourite.[11] I was introduced to British books for young people and became a great fan of Violet Needham. I went through the entire *Swallows and Amazons* series by Arthur Ransom. I read books for young people by 19th century writers like R. M. Ballantyne and Captain Frederick Marryat. Who were the anonymous librarians who chose so many great books for me? I owe them a debt of gratitude. After a year or two, they stopped substituting and started sending me what I ordered. Was it because my choices were now more mature? I can imagine, in the early days, one of them saying: "Oh, what trash he is ordering. We can find him something better than that to read."[12]

---

11  *Bevis*, written in 1882, has been around for a long time, but I have never personally encountered another *Bevis* enthusiast. So, I was surprised when I read *The Enchanted Places* by Christopher Milne. He has written an entire chapter discussing *Bevis*, a book he kept by his bedside for most of his life. (Christopher Milne, a.k.a. Christopher Robin was the son of A. A. Milne and the owner of stuffed animals which were the inspiration for the characters in Winnie *the Pooh*.)

12  Would I have read as much if my family had had television? There is no way of knowing. Many families in town did have black and white TV sets, but my parents held out until 1961 when I was in Grade Eleven.

In the first term of my Grade Seven year, Mrs. McVicar kept a record of the books we read. Whenever we finished a book we were supposed to tell her. She had a large file card for each of us on which she wrote the title and author. Was this a competition of some sort? I don't remember. I do remember discussing the books with her.

Like most elementary school teachers of that era, Mrs. McVicar had not been to university. She graduated from high school in the 1920s and did a year of teacher training at the Normal School in Manitou.

Today we believe that all teachers should have university degrees. And those of us who teach mathematics often believe that elementary classes should have specialized math teachers, in the same way that many of them have special teachers for music, art and phys ed. There are many elementary school teachers who disliked mathematics in their own student days and inadvertently pass on this distaste to their students.

I generally share those beliefs but my memories of Mrs. McVicar tell me that there are exceptions. Her knowledge of the many subjects she was teaching was extensive. She was clearly a lifelong learner. And she was very good at mathematics. She once told me an interesting story about getting a mark of 100% on her final Grade Ten mathematics exam. It was a provincial exam – we used to call them "departmentals" – which was centrally marked.[13]

---

[13] Her account of this was quite interesting. The supervising teacher had distributed scrap paper which he was not supposed to do. All scrap work was meant to be done on the left hand pages of the answer booklet. That summer, she got a letter from the examination board asking how she had scored 100% without any scrap work. She wrote back explaining what happened. She never heard from them again.

So, yes, it is possible to be an outstanding teacher, knowledgeable in the subjects you teach and not have the paper credentials we value so highly. But it is rare, particularly in today's world.

\* \* \*

When I was in Grade Eight I had no idea that I would one day teach Grade Eight students of my own. But that happened. I have taught mathematics at every level from Grade Eight to first year university. Grade Eight was one of my favourite grades to teach.

The two schools where I taught Grade Eight, Gordon Bell and St. John's-Ravenscourt, streamed their mathematics classes.

The first time I taught advanced Grade Eight students at Gordon Bell, it was a class that was given to me part way through the year. I dutifully went through the fixed curriculum, which is what the teacher before me had been doing. They did well but I do not remember a sense of joy. My second advanced Grade Eight class was very different. The standard curriculum for Grade Eight in those years repeated a lot of topics from arithmetic that had been covered in previous years – topics already mastered by the better students. I decided to move on to algebra instead. It was like magic. The students were engaged and enthusiastic for the entire year.

When I came to St. John's-Ravenscourt in 1975, I was once again given an advanced Grade Eight class. I knew what I wanted to do. I limited course content to four days a week, putting aside Tuesdays for "The Tuesday Problems", a series of challenging questions that they would have a week to solve. The four days were enough to cover all of the Grade Eight curriculum and much of Grade Nine algebra as well. Some years there would be a few students who would work on their own and go far beyond that. It did not bother me having students who were in different places. It was like having more than one grade in a classroom.[14]

In my mind, Advanced Grade Eight Math was not a separate course. It was the beginning of a five year course. Whenever possible, I would keep the class intact at the end of the year and move up a grade with them, as Miss Jack had done with my class so many years ago. I kept many of these classes until they graduated from high school, teaching the same students five years in a row. We would complete all of high school mathematics and more in the first four years. After that we did university level courses. Arrangement with a local university allowed them to write examinations and get credit for their work. But it was not all about getting credits. More importantly, it was about learning

---

14  Earlier, I described Grade Eight as a time when certain students absorbed knowledge like a sponge, learning at a rapid pace. Here is an example from my teaching experience: I once gave an advanced Grade Eight student the task of finding the minimum value for a quadratic function. I planned to give him some time to experiment with it, and perhaps graph it. Then I would go on to show him how to do it algebraically. Instead, he immediately solved it by using the derivative – which he mispronounced, calling it the *deri-ative*.
"Who taught you calculus," I asked.
"I learned it from a book," he said.
I was soon to learn that his knowledge of calculus was roughly that of a first year university student. He could not pronounce all the words, but he thoroughly understood the concepts. (A few years later, he amused me again by using the word *monotonous* when he meant *monotonic*.) At the end of his Grade Eight year, I looked through the mathematics section of our school library. Each book had a pocket with a card showing the names of the students who had checked out the book. I discovered that he had checked out almost every mathematics book in the library. For him, the middle school years were a very rich time. Three years later, as a Grade Eleven student, he came first in Canada in the Canadian Mathematical Olympiad, and went on to win a medal at the International Mathematics Olympiad.

how to think mathematically and how to solve problems. They won prizes and honours in numerous mathematics contests. Over the years, several of them were among those chosen to represent Canada in the International Mathematics Olympiad.

With the regular stream of Grade Eight the pace was different. But one thing was much the same. I wanted them to develop a strong number sense. Knowing the basic addition and multiplication facts was a start. These are reinforced when they do traditional paper and pencil calculations. But to really acquire a strong number sense, it is important to spend time doing mental arithmetic.

I required them to commit to memory the decimal equivalents of the common fractions with denominators two, three, four, five, six, eight, and ten. I would then have them use mental arithmetic to find others. What is one-sixteenth as a decimal? No, don't reach for your calculator and don't do long division. You know from memory what one-eighth is. Just take half of that in your head and you've got one-sixteenth. What is one-fortieth? It's just like one-quarter but a tenth as much.

Questions like that also emphasize the fact that there is more than one way to do things. I would ask students to convert one-twelfth to a decimal in as many different ways as they could find.

Some math educators today are opposed to memorizing facts, such as multiplication tables. Finding ways to figure things out, they claim, is more important. The examples above have the best of both views. Memorize some things. Use them to figure out other things. I am all in favour of what I call the "well stocked mind." We are all more successful at thinking things through if we have some facts to start out with. I will have more to say about the "well stocked mind" in Chapter X.

# Chapter IV.
## *High School*

My high school experiences were very different from those experienced by most students today. It had to do with the size of the school. For most of my high school years we had a total of three teachers teaching Grades Nine to Twelve[15] in three classrooms. The two smallest consecutive grades shared a room. Since my grade was one of the smallest, we were always put with either the grade above us or the grade below us. Teachers moved from classroom to classroom when the periods changed. I had no idea that most schools did it the other way around, with teachers staying in their room while the students moved.

There was a big change at Christmas time in my Grade Twelve year. That year a few students had joined us from a nearby town, and suddenly the high school had sixty-five pupils – enough to get a government grant for a fourth teacher. For the last six months of

---

15  In rural Manitoba, in my school days, Grades One to Eight were considered to be Elementary School and Grades Nine to Twelve were high school. Junior High Schools, with Grades Seven to Nine, were found only in cities or very large towns. The modern concept of Middle School was unknown, at least to me. A few years before I retired, Manitoba reorganized the schools to make Grade Nine a high school grade in urban and rural schools alike.

my Grade Twelve year my class had a room of its own, something we had not had since Grade Six.

The building, built in 1916, must have been very poorly maintained. Though not yet fifty years old, it was already decrepit when I was there and condemned just a few years later. It originally had six classrooms for Grades One to Twelve but with the arrival of the baby boom more space was needed. A temporary two room wooden building – really just a large poorly heated shed – was built. It was known as The Annex. A third room was later added to this structure.[16] Finally, in 1956, the annex was removed and a proper elementary school with five classrooms was built for Grades One to Six.[17] The 1916 building housed Grades Seven to Twelve.

In large high schools, students group themselves socially in all sorts of ways, associating with those who share some of their interests. It is different in a small school where there can be less than a dozen in a grade, with the same students together year after year. Everyone gets to know everyone else. When it comes to extracurricular activities, being in a small school brings both advantages and disadvantages. The advantage is that anyone who is interested gets to participate. The disadvantage lies in the fact that there is not a depth of talent to draw on. I have my Grade Nine yearbook in front me as I write this. It is very amateurish compared to the yearbooks of the schools where I later taught. It was the same with our annual drama productions. We had a lot of fun but only a few of the actors were very good at it.

---

16 In the 1955-56 yearbook, Mrs. McVicar, who was teaching in the annex, contributed a poem about her students. The opening couplet was: "Now you meet our little group / We spend our days in the chicken coop."

17 I was in the annex for Grade Five, but got to move into the new school for Grade Six. That was the only year of my schooling that I spent in a modern building.

## Fifty Years in the Classroom and What I Learned There

By Grade Ten, I was taking part in almost everything except for sports. I was editor of what later became the school newspaper. I worked on the yearbook. I was on the student council. I was student librarian, I was in the drama production, and I played chess. Three of us formed an informal photography club, developing our own black and white films and saving our money to get ever better cameras and equipment. The closest I ever came to an athletic activity was in Grade Nine when I was in the tumbling club, an activity that was not offered in later years.

My high school years continued to be quite rich academically but not with the intensity of Grades Seven and Eight. The activities I was involved in made inroads into my time, and my pace of reading slowed from around three books a week to three or four books a month.

Maintaining good marks became very important to me when I reached Grades Eleven and Twelve. My sister had paid her own way through university with scholarships, bursaries and summer jobs. I was determined to do the same. That required good marks on the departmental examinations which came at the end of each school year. In Grades Eleven and Twelve these were worth 100% of a student's final mark. As a teacher, I have encountered many students who, like me at that age, were obsessed with getting high marks. It is a practical quality for the ambitious student but it is not always an attractive quality. Much more attractive is the way things were for me in Grades Seven and Eight where I was obsessed with the subject matter and the good marks just happened.

This was a time when the baby boomers were reaching high school age so there was a great demand for teachers. Dominion City School was among the last of small high schools in Manitoba. In a plebiscite, the region twice voted against amalgamating with other districts to form a division.

Not surprisingly, our local school board often had very few responses when they advertised for teachers. Teachers in large schools were paid better. They did not have to teach as many different subjects and even had some prep time. The Teachers Wanted ads in the classified section of the newspapers took up several columns every day. With so much choice, it is not surprising that few qualified teachers applied for the jobs in Dominion City.

So the school board often had to resort to hiring teachers on permit. These were people who did not have teaching qualifications but were given a one year permit to fill a position that would otherwise go unfilled. French teachers, in particular, were hard to find. We did have one or two permit teachers who were totally unsuited for the job and left part way through the year. But on the whole when I look back on it, I am surprised by how many interesting and talented people the school was able to attract.

In my Grade Nine year, John A. Dyck was the principal and a good math teacher. Frank Fiorentino, who taught us French and history, was just starting a long and successful career in education. Arnold Saper, who taught English and Science (as well as tumbling lessons), went on to a distinguished career as an artist and university professor. In Grade Ten, I liked Bill Dueck who taught math, Henry Martens who taught us geography and English Composition, and Jean-Marie Arcand who came in January, replacing an unsatisfactory French teacher who left at Christmas.

In Grade Eleven, we had Nestor Hochglaube for math, physics, and chemistry. He was a permit teacher only a few years older than his students but he was a brilliant man who had lived what seemed to us an extraordinary life. He was a child survivor of the Holocaust. His early years were spent in Belgium, hidden in a Catholic orphanage, while his parents were hiding elsewhere. After he was reunited with his family, they moved to Israel where he finished elementary school. Later, they moved to Montreal. In his Montreal school he was initially placed in Grade Nine with his age group but soon managed to convince the principal that he should be in Grade Eleven. After high school, he was off to university in New Brunswick where he graduated with a science degree. I loved the enthusiasm he had for the sciences and the interesting and intellectually challenging discussions we often had both during and after classes.

In both Grades Eleven and Twelve, we had Gabe Girard for English.[18] He also taught us Grade Eleven history and he was the school principal. He was very supportive of me, and encouraged my interest in becoming a teacher. (More about that will come in Chapter V.) When he discovered that I, along with some friends, had been issuing a monthly newspaper/magazine, produced at home in my bedroom on a jelly hectograph pad he adopted it as the school newspaper and made the school duplicating facilities available to us.[19] When the school board set aside a significant sum for new library books, he handed me some book catalogues and told me to order whatever I felt the library needed. In the summers after I finished high school, when I ran a small tutoring business, he gave me a key to the school allowing me to operate from one of the classrooms.

---

18 Most of my high school teachers stayed for only one year. The notable exceptions were Jean-Marie Arcand who came in January 1961 and Gabe Girard who came in September of 1961. Both were still there in June of 1966 when the Dominion City School District became part of the new Boundary School Division.

19 The first issue of this paper came out on August 4, 1959 which was in the summer between my Grade Eight and Grade Nine years. The print run consisted of four copies – made with carbon paper. By the end of 1959 I had acquired the hectograph pad, purchased in the nearby town of Altona from D. W. Friesen and Sons. That allowed print runs of twenty or more copies. It became the school newspaper near the end of 1961. There were usually eight to ten issues each year, with issue No. 38 released in June of 1963 at the end of my Grade Twelve year. I was recently surprised to see several copies of this paper on display, along with other school related ephemera, at the municipal museum in Dominion City!

John Barsby

When I think of teachers who have been very influential in my life, the first names to come to mind are Viara McVicar and Gabe Girard. But writing this memoir has made me realize that most of my teachers, in one way or another, had a lasting impact on me. Just a few days before writing these words, the obituary section of the *Winnipeg Free Press* announced the death of Arnold Saper. So many memories came back. Tumbling lessons! I could still do the head stand into my 50s, though I would not dare try it now. Word games! He taught us a game which he called iggly piggly – a guessing game where a clue such as "fake horse" would lead to a rhyming answer, in this case "phony pony." He also explained the concept of learning by association, something I later refined and demonstrated to many classes over many years.

In her 1965 book *Armed with a Primer*, Winnipeg educator Sybil Shack describes teachers as the "anonymous immortals". We all leave a little bit of ourselves with the students we teach and in very tiny ways this influence passes down through the generations.

When I read that passage from Sybil Shack, I thought of a young teacher named Miss McIntyre, who came to teach in Upsala, Ontario just under a hundred years ago. She was the first teacher the village ever had. The school, which was just a log hut, opened with five students ranging in age from six to fourteen. I have an old photograph of her standing at the door to her school. She looks to be about sixteen years old.

My father and my aunt were two of her students, and I grew up hearing many stories about Miss McIntyre. My father was the fourteen-year-old in her class. He had not been to school for several years – none was available in that time and place – and considered himself too old to be among her pupils. He agreed to be there only because five students were needed to get the funding to start a school. It was his plan to quietly disappear when things were underway. But Miss McIntyre arbitrarily put him in

Grade Eight and assured him that she could get him through his Entrance[20] if he stayed.

She passed her love of learning on to both my father and my aunt. And she seems to have been a spunky individual. On opening day, when she and her students arrived, they found a padlock on the school door. A local farmer who had provided some materials for the building of the school had not been paid and was determined that the school would not open until he had his money. While he and the board members tried to sort this out, Miss McIntyre and her young charges wandered off. When the adults finally solved their problems and opened the door, they found that school had been in session for an hour. Miss McIntyre had pried open a window at the back of the building and helped her students crawl through the opening. I would like to have known her.

Here is the quote from Sybil Shack in which she speaks of teachers as the anonymous immortals. As you read it, think of Miss McIntyre or think of your favourite teacher from either elementary or high school.

> However small our influence, however little of knowledge and wisdom we leave with our pupils, year by year and class by class we give something of ourselves to the children we teach. We are a little bit of the mosaic of their lives, and through them in imperceptible flecks of colour we pass ourselves down through the generations and are immortalized. Our names are not emblazoned on great books, nor carved on massive buildings, nor brushed on canvas. Our children forget our faces

---

20 Ontario High School Entrance Examinations were very formal examinations written each year by students finishing Grade Eight. These exams were discontinued in 1949.

and our names, but within them carry part of us.
We are the anonymous immortals.[21]

---

21   From *Armed with a Primer*, McClelland and Stewart, 1965.

# Chapter V.
## *The Knock On The Door*
## *– Teaching At Age 19*

I graduated from Dominion City School in 1963 and went on to take a science degree at the University of Manitoba. I will resist the urge to write about my time at university. That is beyond the scope of this undertaking. It is relevant, however, to say that the transition from a very small school to a university with many thousands of students was not easy. In high school I had an identity. Everyone knew who I was. In university, I was just one in a large mass of people. It took me a few months to be comfortable with such anonymity.

When first year was over, I looked for a summer job with no success. I returned to Dominion City, did some volunteer work at the school (I directed one of the plays for the spring drama production) and started a tutoring business. I placed an ad in the Emerson Journal, so I ended up with students from both towns. I tutored mostly mathematics, physics, and French, but I had a Canadian history student as well.

There were two busy times for tutoring: the weeks leading up to the June exams and the weeks leading up to the August "supps". These supplementary examinations were second chances for students who failed in June. They were also written by summer school students taking a course for the first time.

My tutoring experience turned out to be very useful. Working one-on-one with students who are struggling is a very good way for a future teacher to learn what pitfalls and difficulties students can encounter. Almost everyone I tutored managed to pass the exams and a few did quite well. But I felt like a failure. Some of my university friends had "real jobs" and I had been unable to find one. The world has changed. Today the student who creates his own job would be considered very enterprising but in 1964 I felt as if I had been found lacking.

By my second year I was quite comfortable in university life. I had decided to specialize in mathematics and was in the honours program. One evening in early April of 1965, I was in my room in the Taché Hall Residence when there was a knock on the door. It was exam time and the residence building was unnaturally quiet. My calculus textbook was open in front of me but my mind was not on it. Instead, I was thinking of the summer that lay ahead. I had registered with the student employment office on campus but nothing had come of it. It looked as if it would be another summer of tutoring. I wanted something different, something that would be more exciting – and maybe more profitable!

I opened the door. There, standing in the hallway, was Gabe Girard, my high school principal. He was later to become a school superintendent and later still an MLA in opposition to the Schreyer government. But, in 1965, all that lay in the future.

I was startled to see him there. I asked him in and offered him my chair. Instead, he sat on the edge of the bed. He came straight to the point. The high school science teacher in Dominion City who had been teaching on permit would be leaving early to enter a summer teacher training program. When my exams were finished, would I be willing to take over his position for the rest of the school year?

My reaction was one of total disbelief. I was not an expert on Department of Education regulations but I knew this was impossible. To teach, you had to have a teaching certificate or a permit. Schools could hire permit teachers only if qualified teachers were unavailable. In May, there were large numbers of newly qualified education graduates waiting for their first jobs. There was no chance that the Department would offer me a permit. I said as much.

He told me that he had it all worked out. He had spoken with the local inspector of schools and also the chairman of the school board. As far as the Department was concerned, the current science teacher would be staying until the end of June and the school district would pay him accordingly. This teacher would then unofficially pay me. The inspector, who was responsible for enforcing regulations, had agreed to turn a blind eye to this irregularity. Gabe Girard chose me, he said, because I knew the school, I knew the curriculum, and I knew many of the students.

I did not hesitate. The subjects involved were physics, chemistry, and general science. Although my specialty was mathematics rather than physical sciences, I accepted on the spot.

So, by the first of May I was back in my old high school. Facilities were very primitive, even for those days. The science lab did not have gas, so spirit lamps were used instead of Bunsen burners. Nor was there running water. Water for lab work came from a galvanized tank with a spigot at the bottom. Lab wastes went into a slop pail. The school basement had chemical toilets which were pumped out occasionally, usually after the smell had become unbearable. For washing hands, there were tin basins sitting in a steel trough with a drain. A lift pump with a long handle delivered ice cold water from a cistern under the floor. There was no central bell system. When periods changed, a senior student, designated as bell ringer, stood in the hallway ringing a hand bell.

John Barsby

We did not know it but those were the dying days of the Dominion City Consolidated School District No. 45. Just a few months later, in December 1965, the school would be condemned as a fire trap. Students would finish that school year squeezed into makeshift classrooms in the basement of the United Church. Dominion City and surrounding towns would finally amalgamate to form the Boundary School Division with Gabe Girard as its first superintendent. Two modern new high schools would eventually be built, one in Dominion City and one in Vita. But all that lay in the future. In the spring of 1965 when I returned to my old high school, everything was very much the same as it had been when I left.

So, at the age of nineteen, I began my career as a high school teacher. Some of the Grade Twelves were almost my age. We had been students together just two years previously. One of them was a good friend of mine. It was my job to prepare these students for the departmental exams in physics and chemistry. They addressed me by my first name, which was fine with me. There were no discipline problems. Having a do-or-die examination around the corner kept everybody working.

The Grade Elevens were also very co-operative. They carefully avoided addressing me, either by first name or by "mister". The Grade Nines and Tens were more spirited and turned out to be a lot of fun. They addressed me as they would any other teacher. The Grade Nine course was mostly botany. I had not encountered this material since I had been in Grade Nine myself but I became quite interested in it. Over half a century later I still remember many of the facts presented in their textbook. Facts were what it was all about! The departmental exam for that course consisted of one hundred multiple choice questions.[22] I drilled them day after day

---

[22] When I was in Grade Nine the exam was a traditional long answer paper. A few years later it became a machine marked multiple choice

on everything in the text, including footnotes and captions under the pictures. A modern day science teacher might cringe at this but they did well on the exam.

The days were very busy. There were four high school teachers, including the principal, and four classrooms of students so none of us had any prep time. The last two weeks were easier since Grades Nines and Tens stopped coming in the middle of June when their exams were finished. I spent some of that "free" time making guest appearances in Mrs. McVicar's Grades Seven and Eight room where I did a number of lab demonstrations, including making an ammonia fountain. Her students impressed me with their sense of excitement and enthusiasm. It reminded me of the days when I was a student in that very same classroom.

By June 30th, only the students in Grades One to Eight remained at school. We ended the school year with a flag lowering ceremony. The students stood in rows in the school yard while the Red Ensign[23] was lowered for the last time. Gabe Girard asked me to give a short talk on the history of the flag, which I did, lifting the information from *The Encyclopedia Canadiana*.[24] The

---

paper. It was discontinued in 1967.

23 Manitoba schools had traditionally flown the Union Jack, not the Red Ensign, but in September of 1964 the Conservative government in Manitoba had mandated that schools start flying the Ensign instead, probably to support the federal wing of their party. Flags had become a big political issue throughout most of 1964. The Progressive Conservative party, led by Diefenbaker, wanted to keep the Red Ensign as the Canadian flag and tried very hard to stop the Pearson Liberals from adopting the Maple Leaf flag that is so familiar to us today. They staged a filibuster that went on for a very long time. But the new flag was finally approved and became Canada's official flag on February 15th 1965.

24 This ten volume reference work, published in 1958, used to be in most Canadian school libraries. A revised edition was never published, and it is now long forgotten.

new Canadian flag had been adopted several months earlier but the Manitoba government had asked schools to keep flying the Ensign until the end of the school year. I have often wondered if Dominion City School had another ceremony in September when the new maple leaf flag was raised.

In those two months, I learned a lot about teaching. I learned that it was very hard work and could be totally exhausting. I remember falling asleep one evening, sitting in a chair watching television. When I woke up it was the middle of the night and television had gone off the air for the day. But I also learned that teaching could be exhilarating and very satisfying. I took great pleasure in the students' achievements. I began to realize how important the work of a teacher is, how much influence he or she can have on the lives of the students. I particularly enjoyed working with both Gabe Girard and Viara McVicar who were teachers I admired very much. I never did manage to address them by their first names. Nor did I ever tell them just how important they were in my life. But I think they knew.

That teaching job took me to the end of June, so I still did some tutoring after that. I had an interesting contract that summer with one of the elementary school teachers. This was also arranged by Gabe Girard. He was a young teacher in his mid-twenties who had gone to teachers' college after high school and now wanted to take university courses to upgrade his qualifications. But in those days a second language was required for university entrance, and he had never managed to pass Grade Twelve French. He had written the examination four or five times, both in June and August over several years but never got much more than 40%.[25] Gabe Girard volunteered me as a tutor.

---

25 His situation was not unusual. Every June and every August one or two adults from the surrounding area would come to the school on the appointed examination day to try once again for a pass. If the

I would be paid $75 if he passed but only $25 if he failed! It does not sound like much today but $75 was quite significant in an era when a full year of university tuition was $450. My student scraped through with 54% and I got the $75. Looking back on it, I am amazed that I was so willing to tutor students in French. I had no ear for the language. I had taken it through to the end of my first year at university but I succeeded at it only because I was good at grammar and learning vocabulary.

Two years later when I graduated from university, it seemed natural to choose teaching as a career. Having once gone down that road, I had no desire to turn back. I had found what I wanted to do.

---

curriculum changed, the Examination Board would make special accommodations for these older students, setting an exam on the old curriculum.

# Chapter VI.
## *Snow Lake, Gordon Bell, St. John's-Ravenscourt*

I graduated from university in the spring of 1967 with a B.Sc. (Hons) degree and two weeks later enrolled in the emergency teacher training program offered by the Faculty of Education to deal with the teacher shortage in rural and northern schools. Sometimes known as the 12-6-6 week program, it consisted of twelve weeks of instruction in the first summer, six weeks the next summer and another six weeks in the third summer, although the final six weeks could be waived if one took a correspondence or evening course before then.

After the first twelve weeks, those enrolled in the program were issued a Letter of Authority[26] and had to find a teaching position. It counted as practice teaching, and had to be outside the city of Winnipeg. After the second summer an Interim Teacher's Certificate was issued. Two additional years of teaching were required to make it a Permanent Certificate.

---

26 A Letter of Authority differed from a Permit. Letter of Authority teachers had partially completed a teacher training course, while Permit teachers had no teacher training.

Not counting my unrecognized time teaching in Dominion City, my career was spent in three very different schools. I was in the northern mining town of Snow Lake from September 1967 to June 1969. I was at Gordon Bell, an inner city Winnipeg School, from September 1970 to June 1975. I was at St. John's-Ravenscourt, an independent Winnipeg school, from September 1975 to June 2004. (In the school year 1969-70, I was back at university completing an M.Sc. degree.)

I also did some substitute teaching. In 1966, I substituted for Gabe Girard who took a few days off to run for political office in the Manitoba election held in June that year. (He was defeated that time but was elected in 1969.) I also substituted occasionally at SJR for several years after I retired.

Snow Lake was a ten hour drive from Winnipeg, much of it on gravel roads.[27] The school was small, with two or three hundred students in Grades One to Twelve. Both the new General Course and the University Entrance Course (in those years the two did not overlap) were offered.[28] It was a time and a place where most students did not finish high school. Jobs were readily available. As a result, the classes in the senior grades were very small. In my first year, my class sizes ranged from four students in 11G English to sixteen students in 10G Mathematics. The class of sixteen seemed very large! I had the Grade Twelves for home room. There were ten of them at first but two dropped out before the year was over.

---

[27] In my years there, Snow Lake was 603 miles by road from Winnipeg. Later, when the new Thompson highway was constructed, that distance was greatly reduced.

[28] The General Course was introduced to Snow Lake School one grade at a time, starting the year before I arrived. In my first year there, it was offered only to Grades Ten and Eleven. The following year Grade Twelve was included.

About half of them were born in 1950, a few were born in 1948 and 1949 and one was born in 1947.[29]

Despite small classes, that first year was probably the most difficult year of my teaching career. I taught courses in English, Mathematics and Science, a total of seven courses. I had exactly one prep period a week. I would wake up Thursday mornings with a warm feeling knowing that today I had a spare. I had to prepare lessons on eight different novels – *Of Human Bondage, Tess of the D'Urbervilles, Sunshine Sketches of a Small Town, Leaven of Malice, Huckleberry Finn, Animal Farm, Watcher in the Shadows, Ethan Frome* – some of which were very long and many of which I had never even read before. There were science labs to prepare and the usual tests and examinations to type up and run off and all the marking for seven different courses.

Our local union representative once asked us to count the number of hours a week that each of us spent on school work. Mine came to well over sixty. I survived the year only because of very congenial colleagues and the enormous support of an excellent principal – Ray LeNeal – another hero of this tale, another individual to whom I owe much gratitude.

The second Snow Lake year could not have been more different. I had been through most of my courses once already. I had materials from the previous year that I could use again. I really liked my classes. It was a wonderful time. (For more details see the chapter of this memoir called Magic in the Classroom.)

At the end of that year I moved on. I wanted to return to university to do a master's degree. Most of the Snow Lake staff – including Ray LeNeal – left that year. Snow Lake was a place where teachers came for a year or two and then moved to less isolated locations. In my second year, when a group insurance program

---

29  I was born in 1945, so some of these students were not much older than I was.

was introduced, the actuaries determined that the median age of the staff was twenty-two. Many of the elementary teachers were eighteen or nineteen, just out of Teachers' College.[30] At twenty-three, I was above the median age.[31]

In an interesting coincidence, when Ray LeNeal moved, it was to be superintendent of the Boundary School Division, with offices in Dominion City. In that job he replaced Gabe Girard, who had just been elected to the Manitoba Legislative Assembly. In the spring of 1969, I received a letter from Gabe Girard asking me if I thought Ray was suitable for the position of superintendent. Not many beginning teachers get to write letters of recommendation for their principals!

Then, after a year back at university, I accepted a job with the Winnipeg School Division, teaching at Gordon Bell, a Grade Seven to Twelve school which, in those days, had over 1200 students.

It was a shock. Both Dominion City and Snow Lake had been very small schools where teachers would know all or most of the students. They were orderly places where every student was in an assigned place every period of the day. Gordon Bell seemed to me at first to be filled with chaos. Students roamed the hallways and could leave the school if they did not have a class. They could be anywhere in downtown Winnipeg. If they skipped a class, it

---

30 The Manitoba Teachers' College offered a one year teacher training course to students out of high school. Until 1958 it was known as the Winnipeg Normal School. In 1965 it merged with the Faculty of Education at the University of Manitoba. The one year training program was discontinued a few years later. The era when teenagers could be hired as fully trained teachers came to an end.

31 Such a youthful staff presented us with a dilemma. At that time, the legal age for drinking alcohol was twenty-one. In October, we had suspended two students for drinking at a school dance. Then, in December, we had a staff Christmas party. Were we being hypocrites if our underage teachers drank at the party?

was up to the teacher, not the principal, to do something about it. When I complained to the vice principal about a very disruptive student his response was, "There is nothing we can do about it." Classes were streamed – Phase One, Phase Two and Phase Three we called them. As a new teacher, I was given mostly Phase Two and Three classes. Phase Three classes, particularly in Grades Eight and Nine, had many students with behavioural problems and a lot of truancy.

Yet, by my second year, this had all become normal. I began to appreciate the fact that we were dealing with a cross section of humanity and that included some students who were leading difficult lives. The wise approach was to do what one could for them, not to make their lives even more difficult. And I finally had some Phase One classes. They were a joy to teach.

Phase Three, particularly at Grade Nine, remained difficult although I learned to roll with the punches and accept them as they were. When one of my students had a temper tantrum, swept the contents of his desk onto the floor, swore loudly and stormed out of the room, I picked everything up but made no comment. When the distraction was over everyone else went back to work. When he showed up the next day, I handed him the things he had abandoned and asked him if he was having a better day. In my first year there, I would have felt the need to hand out some sort of punishment for bad behaviour. But now, I realized that could make his future behaviour worse, not better. He may well have been coping with serious problems in his life, problems that I had never had to deal with at his age. If I took any action, it was to suggest that he have a chat with a guidance counsellor.

But I did run into a big problem at Gordon Bell. I took on too many things. My days became very busy and very long. Some Phase One students finished their Grade Twelve Math in Grade Eleven, so I started teaching a course in university calculus, a course that would give them credit at the nearby University of

Winnipeg. The first year that I did this, it was over and beyond my normal teaching load. I wanted the class to get as many As and A+s as possible when they wrote the university exam in April and we worked hard at this.

I also got deeply involved with running two after school math clubs, one for senior high and one for junior high. Our main activity was preparing for mathematics contests. In 1972 we worked very hard getting ready for the Junior Mathematics Contest[32] – forerunner to a number of contests now offered by the Centre for Education in Mathematics and Computing at the University of Waterloo. There were some very good students, and a lot of enthusiasm. I hoped we could win the plaque for highest standing in our Zone[33] and even dared to think that we might have a chance at the Manitoba Championship. The contest was written on March 1st. Then, one day in April, the principal received a phone call telling us that we had placed first in Canada, competing with almost a thousand schools, I was ecstatic. We had never thought of that as remotely possible. Buoyed by this success, we worked even harder at it the next year and won the Canadian Championship again in 1973.

At the same time I was coaching Reach for the Top,[34] and there, too, we started winning. We were Manitoba champions two years in a row. We went to Newfoundland for the national finals in 1974

---

32  This was not a contest for Junior High students. It was for students in Grades Nine, Ten and Eleven. It was the forerunner of today's Pascal, Cayley and Fermat contests.

33  The province was divided into ten zones (or districts). The Manitoba Association of Mathematics Teachers gave a plaque to the top school in each zone. Gordon Bell was in Zone 10, a zone which consisted of all schools in the Winnipeg School Division.

34  Reach for the Top, run by the CBC, was a televised general knowledge quiz game in which teams from participating schools competed against each other.

and to Vancouver in 1975. In Vancouver we kept winning until the final game for the Canadian championship where we were defeated by Queen Elizabeth School from Halifax. Every year we started practicing in late August. Our first game could be as early as September. The playoffs for the Manitoba championship were in June. The national finals were in July. I know of no other competitive activity where the season can be almost twelve months long.

Every afternoon, after classes were over, I stayed at the school, either for Reach for the Top practice or for one of the two math clubs. It was usually well after six before I got home and much later than that before I finished marking and lesson planning. At night I was too wound up to sleep. I would lie awake, my mind racing, thinking of all the things that needed to be done the next day. It seemed impossible to cut back. The activities were too exciting and exhilarating and the students too appreciative. I was back to the sixty hour work week, enjoying every minute of it but totally exhausted. Part of me realized that this was not sustainable. I could not do this year after year after year.

During my fourth year at Gordon Bell, the mathematics department at the University of Winnipeg scheduled occasional meetings for everyone teaching the first year calculus course. That included several high school teachers who had classes of advanced students. One of these high school teachers was Don Johnson, from St. John's- Ravenscourt. He told me that an SJR math teacher would be retiring in June of 1975. He encouraged me to apply for the position when it came up. I had almost two years to think about it.

The idea was tempting and became even more tempting once I was into my fifth year at Gordon Bell. In my third and fourth years I had been given timetables that did not include any Phase Three classes but now a new department head had been appointed who decided that all math teachers had to have their share of the difficult students. In my fifth year, I once again had a Grade Nine Phase Three Class which contained a few students whose behaviour was unpredictable. I was much more comfortable with difficult students than I had been when I first came to Gordon Bell but I still found it stressful. This made the prospect of going to SJR – a place that did not have Phase Three – more attractive. It also would be an opportunity to drop Reach for the Top. I had enjoyed RFTT very much but something had to go.

So I resigned from the Winnipeg School Division and accepted a position at SJR, starting in September of 1975. I steeled myself for a difficult first year. It had been that way at Snow Lake and at Gordon Bell. I had decided that getting used to a new school was always difficult and this would be the same. But it was not. I felt like I was coming home. It was like a combination of Dominion City and Snow Lake but with a lot more students. Everything was orderly and predictable. The headmaster – John Schaffter – was enormously supportive. He, too, is one of the heroes of this memoir and among those to whom I owe much gratitude.

The first few years at SJR were very exciting. There were only three mathematics teachers in the Upper School and we worked together very well. Don Johnson's students had done well in the mathematics contests before I arrived. John Schaffter was advertising the school as a place of academic excellence and found these results very useful in promoting this image. He wanted more of the same. Fortunately, there were some very good students at SJR who loved mathematics and together we worked very hard at it. In 1976 one of our Grade Eleven students was the individual Canadian champion in the Junior Mathematics Contest. In 1977, 1978 and 1979 our teams came first in Canada in that contest.

John Schaffter – who, himself, knew little about mathematics – was a great help in this. Not long after I arrived, he told me that, if we had good contest results, he would shout about them from the rooftops. That is exactly what he did. He took out ads in newspapers to publicize the contest results. These ads appeared not only in Winnipeg but also in rural Manitoba, in Toronto and in Montreal.

In the spring term of 1976, he looked over the national, provincial, and district honour rolls and found we had about forty students listed. He invited them all – and their parents – to a huge party at his house. Members of the board of governors were also there. It took the form of a potluck dinner followed by awards. His wife, Anne, spent days phoning parents and telling them what to bring. It was a wonderful celebration. The praise and prizes heaped upon the winners reminded me a little of the adulation given to football players in the Winnipeg public schools[35] – but this was for math students rather than jocks! There was a sense of excitement in the air. The younger students – those in Grades Eight, Nine or Ten – were determined to do even better when writing the contest next year. That inspiration likely contributed to our winning the JMC in 1977, 1978, and 1979 and in the fourth year, 1980, winning the Canada wide Euclid Math Contest for Grade Twelve.

We continued to do well in the contests over the years. The enthusiasm was less intense after John Schaffter left but the heads of school that followed him remained very supportive. Every year we had a solid group of talented and dedicated math students.

---

35  In 1974 when I was at Gordon Bell their football team – the Panthers – came first in the city, in a league consisting of ten schools. The year before the Gordon Bell math team had placed first in Canada beating out nearly a thousand other schools. I did not resent the fact that it was the football players and not the math students who were paraded through the hallways and made out to be heroes. I took it for granted that this was the way it was. John Schaffter, on the other hand, envisioned a world where winners would receive equal amounts of glory, whether it was mathematics, football, hockey, or something else. Somehow, he was able to bring it about. When he left SJR he did the same thing at St. Michael's University School in Victoria.

## John Barsby

In 1982 the Junior Math Contest morphed into three separate contests, one for each of Grades Nine, Ten and Eleven. The idea of being Canadian Champions was somewhat diluted since each grade had its own championship team. Nonetheless, in the years that followed, we did have a few teams and a few individuals who placed first in Canada in some of these contests. At a more local level, we were almost always the Manitoba champions.

Our strength grew in the more senior contests. We had some very good results in the Canadian Mathematical Olympiad and, over the years, we had several students chosen to represent Canada in the International Mathematical Olympiad.[36]

It should always be remembered, however, that these contest standings show only the achievements of the top students in the school. Don and I and the many fine mathematics colleagues who joined us as the school grew, wanted to create a powerful math program for everybody, not just the students in the Advanced Class, which was the equivalent of Phase One at Gordon Bell. We made calculus an option for any student in Grade Twelve. There was a year in the 1990s when almost the entire Grade Twelve class was taking it. The Advanced Class took University of Manitoba courses in calculus and linear algebra. The other students took a calculus course along with their regular Grade Twelve mathematics. They could take the A.P. Calculus course (examined by Educational Testing Services in the United States) or take a half-credit course which was loosely based on a provincial curriculum. There was also a half-credit course called Advanced Topics which was taken

---

[36] Each year Canada sends a team of six students to complete in the IMO. They are selected on the basis of performance in earlier math contests. SJR had a student chosen in each of 1987, 1991, 1993 and 1996. The SJR student who competed in 1993 won a gold medal. The 1996 competitor won bronze.

by the majority of students. Later, we were able to also offer an A.P. course in statistics.

SJR grew and changed a lot during my twenty-nine years there. In some ways it became a little more like Gordon Bell had been. A time came when students could sign out during their spare periods and leave the campus. A time came when they could sit wherever they wanted at lunch time, rather than at an assigned table. Interactions between teachers and students became less formal. When I arrived, many teachers expected their students to stand up when the teacher entered the room. By the time I retired, this practice had largely disappeared. To me, all these changes were changes for the better.

When I went to SJR, I had no intention of staying for twenty-nine years. I wonder sometimes if that was the right thing to do. In the 1950s and 1960s teachers moved frequently. Jobs were easily available and new experiences were attractive. As teachers gained experience, they were able to apply for better paying jobs at schools where the teaching conditions were better. I have no reliable statistics to back this claim but I suspect that the teachers who retired in the 1960s had taught, on average, at five or six different schools. There is a lot to be gained from this breadth of experience. My Gordon Bell years, for example, were very formative. So much of what I did at SJR was based on what I had learned at Gordon Bell.

I remember with clarity every single year of my teaching career up to about 1990 and then they start to blur together. If I meet a student from the 1980s, I will probably know exactly what year they graduated. I might even remember their classmates and be able to visualize where they sat in the classroom. But if I meet a student from the 1990s, I may be uncertain about their year of graduation. If it is someone I taught for several years I will remember them and remember who their classmates were but if I taught them for only one year there is a small chance I might not remember them at all.

By comparison, I remember the names of all the students who graduated from Snow Lake in 1969. Is this blurring of memory a sign that I stayed at SJR for too long? It was a comfortable place to be. There was never a right time to move on. I always had an Advanced Class that I was keeping together for five straight years and always felt that I had to stay until such a class graduated.

Retirement came sooner than I would have once expected. In my early years of teaching, I saw myself as the kind of teacher who would be pried out of his classroom at age sixty-five. But it is a strenuous job that takes a lot of energy year after year. Eventually, I started thinking of sixty as a more realistic figure.

Then, suddenly in February of 2001, I found myself in hospital recovering from a heart attack and emergency valve replacement surgery. I had none of the usual risk factors, except, possibly, stress. Had those sixty hour work weeks earlier in my career contributed to this?

I decided that the time had come to live a less stressful life. I switched from full time to half time. My youngest students that year were in the Grade Nine Advanced class. Three years of half time teaching brought them to the end of Grade Twelve. They graduated and I retired at the same time. My age at the time was fifty-eight years and nine months. I did some substitute teaching – two or three days a month – for a few years after that but only at SJR and only in mathematics.

# Chapter VII.
## *The Experimental Years At Gordon Bell*

The late 1960s and early 1970s were a turbulent time when many people were questioning traditional ways of doing things. Education was not exempt. Most Canadian provinces were doing away with their provincial examination systems. Methods of grading students – both percentages and letters grades – were under attack. The traditional classroom with one teacher presiding over a class of students was considered a relic of an unsavoury past. Open area classrooms were the wave of the future.

With these new ideas in the air the Manitoba Department of Education had declared Gordon Bell to be an experimental school where many of these ideas would be tried out for a period of five years, starting in September of 1968. What was known as The Gordon Bell Experiment had been in progress for two years when I arrived in the fall of 1970.

I will be discussing some of these innovations in Chapter X. In particular, I will discuss the absence of examinations, the use of a non-traditional grading system, the open area classroom, the use of team teaching, and the concept of Continuous Progress.

Two unusual practices that are not mentioned in Chapter X were rotating classes and the use of IS periods.

Rotating classes occurred because there were not enough open area classrooms to accommodate all the students. When classes were scheduled for the traditional classrooms, teachers were supposed to trade classes at regular intervals. The idea was that students would get to know a variety of teachers. In my first year, for example, I had a Grade Eight Phase Three class until early December. Then the entire team switched classes and I had Grade Eight Phase One until March. Then we switched again and I ended with Phase Two. I did not like it! You barely got to know your students when it was time to give them up.

Then there were the IS periods. Every subject in every grade was given at most five periods in a six day cycle. As a result, every student had two or three spare periods in an eight period day. These were called Independent Study periods. Each department had a designated IS room with a staff member assigned to it. When a student had a spare, he or she could go to any IS room to get help from the teacher on duty or just sit and do homework. But they did not have to do that. They could hang out with their friends in the lunchroom or leave the school.

The Gordon Bell experiment ended in June of 1973 and a lot of these changes were slowly abandoned. Some – like rotating classes and having Phase Three students on Continuous Progress – did not even last until 1973. I stayed until 1975, two years beyond the experiment. By the time I left we had gone back to giving Grade Twelve students marks that were equivalent to traditional letter grades[37]. Grades Seven to Eleven were still receiving report cards where the only grades were superior, pass, or fail which we called the "1", "2", and "3" system.

---

37 A sequence of descriptive words (Honours, Excellent, Good, Average, Pass and Fail) were used instead of the traditional A+, A, B, C, D and F.

One interesting observation about the experimental years at Gordon Bell deals with the way students felt free to follow their passions. I noticed this with Reach for the Top and with Math Club. I am sure the same thing applied to activities such as the annual musical production or sports teams. When the activity became intense – before a big game or a major production – students had no hesitation about neglecting their regular school work and focusing their entire time on the preferred activity. Is there an English essay due? I'll hand it in late or not bother. A math test? I won't study for this one. It doesn't make any difference to my mark, anyway. With a grading system as coarse as "1", "2", and "3" the students were right: one piece of slipshod work would be very unlikely to make any difference. SJR students, on the other hand, were always aware that the one mediocre or missing piece of work could make the difference between a 92% and an 88%. Which is better? A system where students, from time to time, follow their passion and neglect everything else or a system where they must show restraint in following their passion because there is a need to do well in everything all of the time? That's a tough question.

I may sound rather negative about some of the Gordon Bell practices but there was a lot happening that was very good for me professionally. Offering Continuous Progress to Phase One students taught me just how much potential our brightest students have, and how much they can achieve when nobody holds them back. One Grade Ten student completed the math courses for Grades Ten, Eleven and Twelve in a single year. The following year he challenged the first year calculus exam at the University of Winnipeg where he, a Grade Eleven student among hundreds of first year university students, wrote the only perfect paper.[38]

---

38 The professors who taught the course were clearly impressed with his achievement. They gave only one A+ that year, and it went to the Grade Eleven student.

Team teaching taught me the importance of working closely with colleagues. Years later, it was natural for me to introduce the idea to SJR whenever several teachers were teaching exactly the same course. The Phase System taught me the advantages of streaming. The math IS Room was a great resource for both students who needed help with difficulties and also for students who loved mathematics and wanted to spend time there. I had always hoped that SJR could have had something similar, and they did, but not until after I retired. I also learned from the mistakes that Gordon Bell was making. I learned the importance of regular course review, the motivating power of marks, and the importance of staying with a group of students long enough to get to know them.

# Chapter VIII.
## *Teaching Streamed Classes*

Teachers must deal with a wide range of students. At one extreme, there are students who are very successful and highly motivated. At the other extreme there are students who are doing poorly for a variety of different reasons. All of these students should be entitled to the care and attention of a teacher. I have known teachers who declare, with some pride, that they concentrate on the underachievers because the bright students, they say, can look after themselves. There are other teachers who enjoy the intellectual challenge of interacting with their top students and tend to ignore the less capable.

Both the successful student and the underachiever benefit when classes are streamed. But we need to do it right! The lower streams must be places where real learning and improvement happens. And we should always provide an avenue where late blooming students can move to a higher stream.

In this chapter I will discuss my experiences with two very different streams: the advanced math classes at SJR and Grade Nine Phase Three classes at Gordon Bell.

John Barsby

# On the Advanced Mathematics Classes at SJR

In the fall of 2021, I submitted an article to the Globe and Mail in defence of classes for the gifted. These have been increasingly under attack and I wanted the readers to know what happens in such a class. The text of my article appears below. Some of it covers material found elsewhere in this memoir but the ideas are worth repeating.

> Special classes for "gifted" students are currently under attack in Canada. The Vancouver School Board, for example, recently decided to eliminate honours high school courses in math and science for so-called equity and inclusion purposes. I taught such a class in advanced mathematics during the last 29 of my 37 years as a high school teacher – and contrary to today's critics, it was an extraordinarily positive experience for all involved.
>
> The advanced class was a five-year program where the students were tentatively chosen at the beginning of Grade 8. In the early grades, students could move in and out of the class. In later grades, students still had an opportunity to join the class, but usually had to take a summer school course to bridge the gap. Some quite capable students preferred the regular group where they could effortlessly be at the top of the class. Others of equal ability, but with a passion for mathematics, were willing to work very hard to keep their place in the advanced class. We placed students where

they were most comfortable to learn – they were not restricted in any way.

Usually, the class had the same teacher for all or most of the five years. As the years passed a strong degree of group cohesion formed, with the same students and teacher together for so long. The teacher and the students worked together with enthusiasm and a sense of joy.

The advanced class differed from the regular stream in three ways. Most importantly, there was an emphasis on learning to think mathematically – they were regularly being given problems that required original thought and were not just knock-off versions of problems they had seen before. This started in Grades 8 and 9 where one day of each week was set aside for problem solving. Furthermore, the material was covered in greater depth and the pace of the advanced class was also quicker, with students completing Grade 12 mathematics during their Grade 11 year. In their Grade 12 year, they did university-level calculus and linear algebra.

A local university allowed our students to write the final examinations in these courses and receive university credit. Some years a few students chose to work at their own pace, completing their Grade 12 math credit in Grade 10 or even Grade 9. The local university was very helpful, providing professors who were willing to mentor off campus students working independently. A few students graduated from

Grade 12 with as many as five university math credits. It is remarkable how much students who are interested and passionate about a subject can achieve when the opportunities are available.

The achievements of the advanced class students were not limited to passing examinations and earning credits. They also won prizes in provincial and national mathematics contests, both as individuals and as teams. These included a number of Canadian champions. On four occasions, a student from the class was chosen to be on the six member team representing Canada in the International Mathematical Olympiad. One year, when we wrote the American PSAT test, almost the entire class placed in the 99th percentile in mathematics.

I have also taught many regular classes, and, despite what the anti-gifted program critics believe, these were not negatively affected by the existence of an advanced class. It is actually easier to meet the diverse needs of students in the regular class if the ability range is narrower. When students of all abilities are grouped together, the teacher is stretched to help the regular students while also challenging the advanced students. Time is limited, and it is usually the advanced who get neglected. In this way, both the regular and the advanced benefit when there are different academic streams.

I have been retired now for seventeen years, but I frequently encounter former students, now in their 30s, 40s, 50s and beyond, who tell me what a rich experience they had in the advanced math class. What would have happened to these students if they had attended a school that frowned on special classes for advanced students? There would have been a tremendous waste of talent and a lack of joy. We should not deprive our top students of a rich education just so that we can pretend that interest, ability and tenacity are equally distributed among all.

Globe and Mail, October 4, 2021

## On Grade Nine Phase Three at Gordon Bell

In this memoir I have had much to say about the advanced classes I have taught – Phase One at Gordon Bell and the Advanced Class at SJR. To balance this, I should say a little more about the Grade Nine Phase Three classes I had at Gordon Bell in the early 1970s.

At Gordon Bell, the guidance department determined, course by course, whether a student was placed in Phase One, Two or Three. In Grades Ten to Twelve, the students in Phases One and Two took the university entrance courses while Phase Three students took the general courses.[39] In Grades Seven to Nine all phases covered roughly the same curriculum, with a large amount of enrichment in Phase One and an emphasis on the basics in Phase Three.

---

39 The university entrance courses were known by their course numbers: 100, 200, and 300. The general courses had numbers 101, 201, 301.

Phase Three classes, at the Grade Eight and Nine levels, had numerous behaviour problems and a lot of truancy[40]. I eventually got along quite well with these classes but, when there were behaviour problems, I always found it stressful. But that was just me. There are many teachers who are very gifted at handling some of the more difficult students. I can think of a Gordon Bell phys ed teacher who was outstanding in his ability to relate to even the most troubled of teenagers. It requires a heavy dose of what John Millar (see Chapter XII) referred to as Heart Power. It requires one to be part teacher and part social worker. As teachers we all have our strengths and weaknesses.

I was given Grade Nine Phase Three classes twice during my five years at Gordon Bell – in my second year and my fifth year.

There were usually about twenty-five students on the class list and an average attendance of about sixteen or seventeen students. Unfortunately, the students who were present on any given day could be quite different from the students who had been there the day before. There were about a dozen students who were there most of the time, about ten students who attended sporadically, one or two students who rarely attended at all, and a student or two who might have been there in September but who had totally disappeared. Staff members would refer to these non-attending students as "ghosts."

Many students arrived at class without any books or notebooks. They even arrived without having a pen or a pencil.

---

[40] In contrast, by the time students reached Grade Eleven or Twelve the Phase Three classes were quite pleasant, having no problems with either behaviour or attendance. The so-called troublemakers from the earlier grades tended to leave school even before the legal age of sixteen.

The first time I had such a class I struggled for five or six weeks making very little progress. Finally, I talked about it with my department head.

She was scheduled to teach a Grade Eleven class at the same time that I was teaching Grade Nine Phase Three. "Let's trade classes for a week," she said, "and I will straighten them out for you."

And she did! She told my Grade Nines that she was there because I was teaching a special unit to her Grade Elevens – a unit that only I could teach. She told them how lucky they were to have me as a teacher.

"We won't be using your textbooks," she said. "From now on you can leave them in your lockers." She gave them each a manila folder with their name on it. In each folder there were some worksheets and a pencil. In a brief lesson, she showed them what they needed to know for the first worksheet. They went to work. At the end of the class she collected the folders, making sure each one still had the pencil in it. Later in the day, she had a chance to look through the folders and gave each student a mark on what they had done.

The next day she briefly taught the same lesson again, for the benefit of those who had not been there the day before and went on to teach the material for the next worksheet. This continued with a new worksheet each day.

After a few days I took over. I continued with the folders and the worksheets for the rest of the year. The class made considerable progress. It took some time to prepare a new worksheet for every class but the effort was worth it. I did find the daily marking rather onerous but I realized it was a very important part of this system. Knowing that the worksheet would be collected at the end of the period and marked, kept most of them on task all period long.

In my final year at Gordon Bell, when I was given Grade Nine Phase Three again, I knew exactly what to do. I got some pencils and some manila folders and made some worksheets. But I was not going to spend about forty-five minutes a day doing the marking. I was already putting in close to a sixty hour work week. So I found a Grade Twelve student who would do the marking for me. He made a sheet for each folder, showing students their daily marks, and kept a spreadsheet for me with everybody's marks. At the end of every unit we had a test. Each student received a unit mark which was the average of their test mark and their folder mark.[41] After they had written the test they could empty their folder and we would start a new unit. My marker was paid a modest amount. The school budget had some funds for markers, but not for mathematics. If I remember correctly, he was paid from the Business Ed budget. After I left Gordon Bell, the manila folder system for Grade Nine Phase Three continued for a few more years – using the worksheets that I had already prepared and paying the same marker who by that time was a university student.

---

41  I gave them traditional percent marks for each unit. But, at report time, I still had to grade them on the "1", "2", "3" grading system that Gordon Bell had introduced during the experimental years. Over 80% earned them a "1" and over 50% earned them a "2". The motivating power of the daily feedback might have been even stronger if their marks had remained as percentages.

# Chapter IX.
## *Magic In The Classroom*

There is something magical that sometimes happens in the classroom. Rarely have I heard teachers talk about it or discuss it but most of us have encountered it at one time or another. This magic unfurls when a strong bond develops between the teacher and the class. There is a kind of group cohesion where everyone works together with enjoyment and enthusiasm and a unity of purpose. The teacher inspires the students and they in turn inspire the teacher. This upward spiral results in great things.

I discovered it in my second year of teaching, in Snow Lake, with the seven Grade Twelve students who were in the academic stream that year.[42] I spent a lot of time with them since I was both their English teacher and their mathematics teacher. They were also in my home room, along with the six other Grade Twelves who were in the non-academic stream.

In the spring time, we faced the departmental examinations as a team. It was they and I together against the big bad examination

---

[42] That was the first year that students were allowed to choose courses from either the University Entrance stream or the General stream but only one Snow Lake student did so. In later years, the distinction between the two streams vanished as students chose some courses from one stream and some from the other.

board. We finished the courses early enough to have several weeks to go over old examination papers. I made my classroom available to them in the evenings so they could have a quiet place to study. My colleague, Murray Colp,[43] who taught physics and chemistry was also caught up in the magic spell. He and I were there every evening to help them one-on-one as needed. Most evenings the entire class – all seven of them – were there.

After two or three hours of studying, the nine of us would go out for something to eat at a nearby café before going home to bed. The magic resulted in phenomenal examination marks. It resulted in scholarships.[44] It resulted in six out of the seven students going to university the next year, most being the first in their family to ever do so. Of the six who went to university, two became engineers. One became a teacher. One, with a degree in biology and a love for the outdoors, became a conservation officer. One became a medical doctor, first working in general practice, and later becoming a psychiatrist. One I lost track of. These were among the first – if not the very first – students from Snow Lake to ever go to university.

I have seen this magic happen many times since. When it doesn't happen – and that is most of the time – all is not lost. The curriculum is covered, assignments are set and marked, exams

---

43  Murray later joined the staff at SJR so we were colleagues there as well.

44  One of the students won the prestigious Isbister scholarship. Several were awarded Manitoba Government bursaries. Two of them won Hudson's Bay Mining and Smelting Company (HBM&S) Scholarships. These were full scholarships offered to the top two students who attended school in either Flin Flon or Snow Lake, based on departmental exam marks. In the past, these scholarships had always gone to Flin Flon, a much larger town. In 1969, both winners were from Snow Lake. HBM&S was persuaded to give out a third scholarship that year so that Flin Flon would also have a winner.

written and graded, and credit given. All is satisfactory but lacking in the excitement and joy and heightened achievement that the magic brings.

In my first year at Gordon Bell, I encountered the opposite phenomenon. It was a Grade Ten class. We did not have a designated classroom. We met wherever there was room. Once a cycle we were scheduled, along with four other classes, to meet in the school lunchroom, one class in each corner. There was no blackboard and no screen for an overhead projector. Students from all grades were accustomed to hanging out in the lunchroom when they had spares, so we needed one teacher to guard the door, telling outsiders that the room was out of bounds that period. Getting the students to work was difficult. That group of students became one that I dreaded no matter what room we were in, and I am sure that they dreaded me equally. By the end of that year my memories of magic were growing dim.

But magic did come again starting with my second year at Gordon Bell. It came in advanced math classes that challenged university exams and Reach for the Top Teams that I coached. I particularly remember the magical hour once a week after school in 1974 when the senior math club did what we called The Thursday Problems. This was my first attempt at a general problem solving seminar, rather than one aimed at preparing for a specific math contest. Very few of the attendees ever missed a session. There was a wonderful feeling to it. Most of the students were from Phase One math classes but a few were from Phase Two. In time I noticed that while these students did not contribute a lot to the discussion, they were taking it in and started doing better and better in their regular math classes. They were learning to think rather than just mastering a collection of type problems. I learned that problem solving was for everybody, not just for those in the advanced stream. At SJR, I incorporated it into class time rather than doing it as an after school activity.

Then came my twenty-nine years at SJR. There I encountered the magic many times. Some years it was a pervasive magic that seemed to be everywhere. Some years it was more elusive. I had once hoped that, with age and experience, I would learn to summon it at will but that never happened. Every class has a personality of its own, a kind of group dynamic. Some seem to provide fertile grounds for magic and some do not.

The advanced classes that I stayed with for five consecutive years, from Grade Eight to Grade Twelve were almost always fertile grounds for magic. The group dynamics were excellent. They worked hard. They wanted to please me. I wanted to please them. Math class was a place where they were very comfortable, surrounded by like minded friends – friends they had been with for many years. Every September we picked up where we left off with no time wasted getting to know each other. I look back with some amazement at how much they achieved and how much enjoyment they had along the way.

But I must not give the impression that magic only happens in advanced classes with very bright students. For a few years, in the early 1980s, we did a three way split with our Grades Ten to Twelve mathematics students, separating them into the Advanced Class, a strong regular class, and the weaker students who might need a little more help.

I took the bottom Grade Tens one year. These were all students who had had less than 70% in their Grade Nine math course although some were quite good in other subjects. I did not expect it to be a place where magic would unfold. Nor did I expect to learn a teaching technique that I was to use for the rest of my career. But both things happened.

About three weeks into the year, after completing the first unit, I gave them a test. Many of them did poorly. I took a whole period to go over the test. I told them that we would no longer have unit tests. Instead, we would have a test every cycle, and that test would be cumulative, going back to the beginning of the year. If a question was badly done, a similar question would occur on the next test and probably on the one after that. I taught new work on four days of the six day cycle, tested on the fifth day, and went over the returned test on the sixth.

Their marks went up and up. Returned tests were taken home and studied carefully, not just shoved into the debris at the bottom of a locker. They delighted in their improvement and took pride in their work. Many of them had 80s and even 90s by the end of the year. I kept them together and took them for Grade Eleven as well. I would have seen them through Grade Twelve if timetabling had permitted it.

This magic happens in many classrooms in many schools, yet I never hear educators talking about it. The evidence is everywhere. There are schools that win disproportionate numbers of awards in science fairs or excel in mathematics contests or turn out prize winning public speakers and debaters or consistently produce winning athletic teams. These are all places where magic is unfolding.

Educational researchers rarely visit these schools to find out how it happens. When Gordon Bell – an inner city school – placed first in Canada in the Junior Mathematics Contest, no educational researcher ever came to see how we did it. Instead, they study easier things, like the use of technology in the classroom and new methods of course delivery. Sometimes they suggest that those of us who are now retired spent our careers doing it all wrong.

Some of them should look into magic. They would likely want to give it a less whimsical name but somebody might be able to find out how and why and when it happens – and why it sometimes fails to happen in the best of classes. Magic on demand! That would really revolutionize education.

# Chapter X.
## *Observations And Opinions On Assorted Topics*

Here are some thoughts and opinions on a variety of educational topics. On many of these topics, my opinions changed with age and experience. I sometimes cringe when I remember how naïve I was at the beginning of my teaching career. I saw many issues in stark black and white terms, which later on turned out to be better viewed in numerous shades of grey. My younger self would have disagreed with some of these opinions. But they are the ones I hold today.

## On Student Marks

In my student days, and in my early years as a teacher, students received percentage marks. In 1970 when I went to Gordon Bell, the school had permission from the Department of Education to abandon traditional marks in favour of a three-point system: Students received a grade of 1, 2 or 3, where 1 was given for superior work, 2 for satisfactory work and 3 for unsatisfactory work. When I went to SJR in 1975, the exams and report cards were all done in traditional percentage marks but the transcripts that went to universities were in letter grades.[45] A few years later, in an attempt to make grading comparable from one school to another, the Department of Education required all schools to use percentages. So SJR transcripts had to abandon letter grades.

Which is the ideal system? I don't think there is a clear answer to that. All I can say with certitude is that percentage marks are more fun than the alternatives. For a strong average student, it is boring to get a B time after time. But getting a 75% followed by a 78% gives the illusion of progress. It holds the promise of getting an 80% next time. The Gordon Bell system was very boring. Many students got a 2 in every single course, year after year. They knew that they could get a 2 with very little effort. If they worked a lot harder, the chances are that it would still be a 2. It did not provide a lot of encouragement.

But what does a percentage mark mean? In my student days, when final exams were often worth 100% of the final mark, it was clearer. If you had 75% it meant that you knew 75% of the course content. Of course, that, too, was an illusion. You could have written a different exam on the same material on a different day and easily had 70% or 80% depending on whether the questions asked matched the topics you knew the most about. But we felt we knew what marks meant.

Then came a time when marks were based not only on exams but on term tests and hand-in assignments as well. You could be penalized if your assignments were late. You could be given a zero on an assignment if you plagiarized. So now your mark reflects not only what you know but also your tendency to procrastinate and even your morality. It also reflects whether you are a tortoise or a hare. Some students beginning in a totally new area of study

---

45 This allowed us to make sure that different subjects had similar marks. An A in mathematics might be any mark over 86%, while an A in English might be any mark over 75%.

– calculus for example – might struggle at first, getting a few poor test marks. Then they have that sudden epiphany when everything falls into place – it all makes sense – and they get nearly 100% on the final exam. In the old days that exam mark would have been their final grade but now they will be penalized for that slow start.

This does not mean that I am advocating a return to the days of the 100% final. The disadvantages of that are clear and obvious. But we should be aware that interpreting the meaning of a mark is not as easy as it once was. I also suggest that teachers should have some leeway in how they calculate final marks so that students who get off to a slow start still have a chance of getting a very good mark in the end.

To make things more complicated, until recently there were different scales for different subjects. Students in subjects like mathematics or physics often got marks in the 90s and it was even possible to get 100%. In English, very few students got marks above 80%, and 90s were unheard of. English teachers justified this by observing that any student essay could always be better. Perfection was not attainable. But was that not also true in mathematics or physics? It all depended on what was asked. I could easily set a mathematics examination in which the very best of my students would have trouble breaking 80%. It was just not traditional to set such examinations.[46]

---

46  As I write this, I am reminded of two years in the 1980s when the Canadian Mathematical Olympiad was unusually difficult. It is meant to be a very challenging mathematics contest but in those years the examiners succeeded in making papers so difficult that the median score was zero. There were 200 students invited to write, based on the results of earlier mathematics contests. The examiners had taken the 200 brightest and most promising mathematics students in Canada and set a paper so hard that half of them could not score a single point.

That disparity between mathematics marks and English marks has largely disappeared. Marks have increased in all subjects but the greatest upward trend has been in English marks. Today it is possible for students to get 100% in English just as it is in mathematics.

This mark inflation has happened slowly over the years. In 1963, my high school graduation year, an average of 85% would have placed a student in the top 1% of the province. The very highest average in Manitoba that year went to a Winnipeg student with just over 90%.[47] In my last year of teaching the top two students at SJR had averages of almost 99%. Occasionally, I will read a newspaper account of some scholarship winner who graduated with an average of 100%. This would have been unthinkable a generation or two ago.[48]

Many teachers lament mark inflation but if we do not go along with it our students are at a disadvantage when applying to university. Did mark inflation begin with schools giving higher marks or did it start with universities requiring higher marks for admissions and for scholarships? I don't know the answer to that question. It's a lot like the famous question about the chicken and the egg.

---

47  He attended Kelvin High School. I got to know him in my first year at university since we were in the same chemistry lab.

48  Some years before I retired an outstanding SJR student applied for a scholarship at a prestigious university. We were surprised when she did not win. Our university counsellor made inquiries. He learned that they did not even read her application materials. They rejected her because she had 89% in English, and they wanted all marks to be over 90%. They did not know that 89% was the highest mark any of our English teachers had ever given. After that, we started giving higher marks in English, and eventually in other subjects as well. That is how mark inflation spreads.

In the higher grades, where students have many options, teachers should be particularly careful about resisting mark inflation. If students know that a very high average is needed to get into the university of their choice, they will tend to avoid taking courses where very few high marks are given. I have known situations where teachers were offering excellent courses to just a handful of students. If they had been a little more generous with their marks, they would have had a full classroom.

I sympathize with the teachers who lament mark inflation but I am not one of them. It simply does not matter. It does not detract from what is really important – and that is the learning that takes place. We do not know what the mark really measures anyway. All we know is that it is some sort of score and that with practice and hard work students will find their scores going up. It is like the score on a video game: hard work and stick-with-it-ness pay off. As long as marks motivate students to do their best and allow them to track their improvement, then they have served their purpose.

## On Standards

Many years ago, I thought I understood this word. I am less sure now. It dates back to a time when credentials were given to students who had shown mastery of a certain body of knowledge. They had met the standard.

But even in the 1960s, when I was taking my courses from the Faculty of Education, a different paradigm was emerging. Elementary school students started to pass from grade to grade even if they were not performing at some fixed standard. Failure was almost a thing of the past. The teacher's task was to take the students from where they were and progress from that point. The end goal was not fixed. If a Grade Eight student was only reading at a Grade Four level in September but had reached the Grade

Six level by June, considerable progress was made. The era when students in Grade Six could be well into their teens was vanishing. In high school, a plethora of new courses were introduced to meet a wider range of interests and ability levels. Today the high school graduation rate is very much higher than it was two generations ago. I have some pass/fail statistics[49] at hand for the year 1960: In June of that year, among the Manitoba Grade Twelve population, only 65.8% passed mathematics. In the two required English courses, 65.4% passed in Drama and Poetry and 74.4% passed in Composition and Prose. Many students must fall by the wayside if rigid standards are to be maintained.

It should also be observed that the old fashioned standard worked in both directions. It defined where a student should be. Teachers did what they could to pull weaker students up to that level but at the same time stronger students were being pulled down to that level. Their needs were simply ignored. In the 1950s there was probably not a single high school student in Manitoba who was proficient in calculus. Today there are hundreds.

So we muddle along with a mixture of the old paradigm and the new. We give standardized tests from time to time to see how, on average, our students are doing. We participate in Canada wide tests that compare our students to those in other provinces and international tests that compare our students to those in other countries. This is all in accordance with the old standards paradigm. But when it comes to the progress of an individual student we are on the new paradigm. We do not fail large numbers

---

49   The Report of the Department of Education for the Year Ending June 30th 1964 gives June exam results for the years 1960 to 1964, both the number of exams written and the pass rates. It also gives the number of August supplementary exams written but it does not give the pass rates. Perhaps that is because the pass rates would be low. August exams were written mostly by weaker students who had already failed the course at least once.

of students in the name of maintaining standards. Nor do we ignore the needs of those who can easily advance far beyond the so-called standard.

## On Streaming

Chapter VIII showed two examples of streamed classes, one for high achievers and one for those who are struggling. It would have been very difficult for any teacher to meet their needs if they had been mixed together.

Streaming has become an unpopular practice in recent years.[50] Curriculum for courses in English and history has gone back to a "one course fits all" model. There is some justification for this. The regular students benefit from rubbing shoulders with the strongest of their classmates. When teachers have high expectations students rise to the occasion, and when expectations are low achievement is also low. All of these things are true but they should not require us to completely abandon ability grouping.

We need to be aware of these issues and mix the students together in as many settings as possible. Home rooms should be mixed. In some subjects – I will make enemies if I name particular ones – streaming may be less essential than in others.

In the lower streams teachers have an opportunity to do remedial work. They should set their expectations at a level that challenges but does not destroy their students. At SJR we had a three way stream for our Grade Twelves. The bottom stream was a place where many students found themselves thriving, after having had a difficult year in a regular Grade Eleven class.

---

50  Streaming is also known as tracking, particularly in the United States. In my years at Gordon Bell the various streams were called phases. I have never heard that term used elsewhere.

For students in the top stream, it often makes the difference between going through school joyfully, and being bored day after day, possibly losing all interest in the subject. Our society should not sacrifice its young people – either the high achievers or those who are struggling – in the name of egalitarianism.

Fortunately, many schools understand this and have not gone along with the "one course fits all" curriculum. Instead they look beyond the province for advanced level courses. Advanced Placement (AP) and International Baccalaureate (IB) courses are very common.

In mathematics, by the time students reach the senior grades, the disparity in knowledge, numerical skills, algebraic skills, and problem solving skills is so vast that it is not possible to offer everybody the same course. In Manitoba, students can take Pre-Calculus Mathematics, Applied Mathematics, or Essential Mathematics. The educational theorists who are opposed to streaming pretend that these are equally rigorous courses. Students, they claim, choose one or another according to their interests, not their ability. The guidance counsellors and math teachers who advise the students on their selection know better and direct the students towards the best course they have a chance of passing.

## On Student Cheating

I almost decided to ignore this topic. It is too depressing. Besides, teachers have long ago learned either to ignore it or to convince themselves that it rarely happens. Two or three times in my teaching career I did a little test to see how pervasive it was. It is an easy test that any teacher can do but I don't recommend it. It smacks of entrapment. But here is what you do. Make two versions of a test, ideally a short answer test. The two tests, unless inspected carefully, should look exactly the same. The questions are almost identical but the answers will be different. Here is an example showing the first three questions on a Grade Ten mathematics test:

## VERSION ONE:

1. The slope of the line $3x + 4y - 8 = 0$ is _____

2. The distance between $(2, -3)$ and $(4, 5)$ is _____

3. If $(2, 3)$ is on the line $2x + 3y - k = 0$ then $k =$ _____

## VERSION TWO:

1. The slope of the line $3x - 6y - 8 = 0$ is _____

2. The distance between $(1, -3)$ and $(4, 5)$ is _____

3. If $(2, 3)$ is on the line $2x + 5y - k = 0$ then $k =$ _____

Distribute the tests in such a way that Version One and Version Two papers alternate as you go up the rows and across the aisles. Then mark the tests, and keep track of the number of times a Version One test has a wrong answer which just happens to be the right answer to the corresponding Version Two question and vice versa. The results might be shocking. If it is a strong class where students are confident and do not feel the need to cheat, you might be able to sleep that night. But if it a class where the motivation to cheat is stronger you will lie awake wondering what to do with or say to the class tomorrow. What will you do with the boy who had a Version One paper but appears to have copied almost every answer from the Version Two paper written by the student in front of him?

Why do some students cheat? Some years ago I had a colleague who was very close to retirement. I will call her Barbara but that is not her real name. She told me a story about her teacher training in the 1940s. She wanted to be a high school teacher. The certification program at that time had a number of compulsory courses. One course involved making pencil drawings of things like flowers and fruit. She was not good at this and did not see how it could help her in the high school subject she wanted to teach. But she had a friend who had previously taken the course and had been quite good at it. Week after week when it came to handing in her assignment, she took her friend's drawing from the year before, erased the name, wrote in her own and handed it in. Barbara did not think of this as cheating at the time. An unnecessary and useless hurdle had been placed in her path and this was a way of getting around it. She had no respect for the course. She felt she should never have been forced to take it. However, in her years as a teacher, she would have been both devastated and indignant if students had handed in work that was not their own. She saw what she was teaching as useful and valuable and cheating on it would have been morally wrong. In her mind, that long ago course was different.

A few years ago, there was a scandal at an American university when it was discovered that almost the entire engineering class had cheated in a course called engineering ethics. The media made much of the irony involved – that ethics of all courses should be the one where they cheated. But to me that made perfect sense. It was like Barbara and the art course. I do not know for sure what the ethics course was like but this is what I suspect: Instead of having an engineer teaching it – someone who could talk about the real life ethical problems that an engineer might encounter – they probably farmed the course out to someone from the philosophy department who taught the same course he would have taught philosophy students. The engineering students simply did not respect it.

Our school system is filled with hurdles that students must get around. It is not as bad today as it once was. Think of the years when a second language was required for university entrance and of the many students with high marks in all their other subjects who never got to go to university. But even today there are a lot of requirements to be met and some students, like Barbara, will find themselves in a course where they have no interest or talent. Universities which demand ever higher marks for entrance do not help. There are many ambitious students who feel that their life will be in ruins if they do not graduate with a 90% average. The temptation to cheat is strong.

So, what do we as teachers do about it? Draconian punishments are not the answer since the crime is pervasive, and we catch so few. The message we want to communicate is "Do not cheat." Severely punishing the very few who are caught tends to communicate a different message: "Do not get caught."

The most important thing we can do is to make sure that students respect our courses. We must not make assignments that have no value, that are mere busy work. As much as possible we should keep the courses interesting and the students engaged.

But, even if we do this, there will be some cheating. Some student who is swamped with work and simply unprepared for a test will be tempted to cheat. All we can do is let the student know that we are deeply disappointed and arrange for him or her to write another test or do another assignment and do it honestly. In handling this, if we allow the student to retain his or her dignity, there is a good chance that it will not happen again. Students want to please the teachers who treat them well.

If a student is caught cheating, many teachers give a mark of zero for the test or assignment where the cheating happened. I do not recommend this. I still like to think that marks are pure, representing what the students know and not a reflection of their morality. As for the students who get the zero, they will feel resentful and will be careful in the future to find ways of cheating that are less easily detected.[51]

Since this has been a very depressing topic, let me end with a positive observation. Despite the prevalence of cheating, the majority of students are still very honest when writing tests and doing assignments. Every year, when I handed back tests or examinations, there would be students who would let me know if I had accidentally given them too many marks. One year a Grade Twelve student was waiting for me outside my office door when I arrived early in the morning. He had written a test the day before. He was among the last to hand it in, struggling with a question that he could not do. Then he overheard two students, who had already handed in their papers and left the room, talking about it outside the door. With what he overheard, he was able to do it himself and handed in his paper. He had a guilty conscience and

---

[51] In the 1969-70 academic year I was a graduate student at the University of Manitoba. I had been hired to do the tutorial sessions for two sections of Mathematics 120, which was a full year introductory calculus course. On the first test two students – brothers for whom English was a second language – handed in papers that were word for word the same. Each paper added up to 74, with exactly the same mistakes in the same places. They had sat at the same table when writing the test. I should have reported this to the professor who was in charge of the course but I felt rather sorry for the offenders who were far from home and trying to function in a language that they were just learning. I confronted them with the evidence. I tentatively gave them each a mark of 37. I told them they could discuss it among themselves, and split the 74 marks any way they wanted. They settled for the 37 each. In subsequent tests I made sure they were at different tables. One of them turned out to be much better at calculus than the other, so it became apparent who had written that paper and who had copied it. That was fifty years ago. Would I have handled it differently today? Probably. But I still would have been reluctant to report them since the official penalties were very draconian.

a sleepless night. He was there early in the morning, to ask me to scribble out his answer to that question so he would not get any marks for it.

## On the Changing Times

Society changes and schools change with it. That is both desirable and inevitable. The schools of today are vastly superior to those of my childhood. They attempt to meet the needs of all their students, not just a few and on the whole do it very well. I look back on my school years with pleasure but what about those classmates of mine who dropped out in Grade Six when they turned sixteen? What memories do they hold of their school days?

There are times, however, when I wish the people advocating one change or another would not do it with such evangelical fervour. Think of the debates on the teaching of reading that were waged throughout much of the last century. Phonics was out and sight reading was in. But a decade later phonics was back again. In mathematics, learning times tables and memorizing facts was out and the discovery approach was in. But today, increasingly, learning multiplication tables is back again. The so-called experts seize on a new idea and promote it as the one and only way to success. Their idea is often good but that does not mean that other approaches were wrong. The good teacher should and does use a variety of approaches. What works best for one student might be a disaster for another.

The same can be said of teachers. Different teachers have different personalities. Things that work for one teacher might not work so well for another. We all have our own strengths and our own weaknesses. We all must find our own way. When I first went to Gordon Bell, the mathematics department head was someone with a commanding presence. She could walk into a large room with a hundred or more noisy students and, with a small gesture of her hand, establish total silence. I envied her that ability but it was something I knew I would never be able to do.

Education consultants and experts should concentrate less on teaching methods and more on the results that teachers get. So often I have heard that smug little aphorism that the modern teacher is "the guide on the side, not the sage on the stage." Good teachers have always been both. When students of mine want to work ahead of the class, of course I am the guide on the side. When the entire class is working on a challenging set of problems, sometimes individually and sometimes in groups, I am there as the guide. But there are also magic moments when there is a sense of excitement in the air as I show them a particularly neat solution to a problem or a very elegant proof to a theorem. At those times it is a joy to be the sage on the stage and a joy to be in the audience. Good teachers do whatever works, whatever produces the desired results.

Some bold new innovations in education have staying power and make the school a better place. Some, like the open area classroom, either fizzle out or evolve into something else. The ones that do not survive can make experienced teachers into cynics.

A young vice principal, filled with enthusiasm, speaks of some new idea that will revolutionize the way we do things. He manages to imply – or outright says – the old way was all wrong. But in the audience, there are teachers who have been around for a long time, who have more experience than this vice principal. They have seen ideas introduced with great enthusiasm only to be abandoned a few years later. They are not impressed with the zeal of the vice principal. "Here we go again," they say to each other.

Equally, the vice principal is not impressed with them. "What will we do with these stick-in-the-mud dinosaurs?" he says to the principal when the meeting is over.

Both are at fault. This vice principal should know that education is a complicated business. Different students learn in different ways, different teachers have different talents, and it is simplistic to embrace one idea as the great panacea that will solve all our problems. But these older teachers, too, are at fault. They should recognize that many of the changes they have seen were, in fact, positive. We all should be open to change for the better and have the wisdom to distinguish it from change for the sake of change.

## On Outcome Based Education

When I first started teaching, the curriculum outlines provided by the department of education were quite brief. The older ones, for courses approved some years previously, were often on a single page. They specified what textbook was to be used and what pages were to be covered. That was about it. The newer ones were sometimes a few pages long, stapled in the corner. They were also based on a specific textbook but, as well as specifying pages to be covered, there was some discussion of the material.

Later, in the 1970s or early 1980s, schools were free to choose their own textbook, so curriculum outlines became very much longer, explaining in detail what topics were to be covered and to what depth.

I am not sure when the outlines first became outcome based. I did not pay a lot of attention to it. But I became very aware of outcomes when I became a member of the western provinces curriculum committee. That first meeting, which took place over several days, in Regina, was a real eye opener.

The leaders of the session were curriculum experts. Some of their demands seemed silly to me and they still do. We could not use headings like algebra, geometry and trigonometry in the high school curriculum because these were not taught in kindergarten.

The headings had to be appropriate for all levels. Geometry had to be renamed as Shape and Space. Algebra became Patterns and Relations. Trigonometry was split between these two. There was a separate category for statistics but I forget what it was called.

Within each topic, the material had to be specified as a series of outcomes. My group had a lot of trouble with this. We would start an outcome with phrases like "Students should understand …" only to be told that was not acceptable. Outcomes must be measurable. We were finally given a list of verbs that could be used. Students could solve, calculate, factor, determine, demonstrate, etc. All these outcomes could easily be tested. We could not say that students should know, understand, appreciate or enjoy. At one point we wanted to say that students should understand the difference between a quadratic function and a quadratic equation. How could we get this past the experts? Finally, we wrote "Students should be able to demonstrate orally or through writing, the difference between a quadratic function and a quadratic equation." That was acceptable.

That was more than twenty years ago. Outcome based education is still with us and will probably be around for a while. It will be perfect in some dystopian future when an AI expert is teaching a class of robots. Until then, it doesn't matter much. The content to be covered is very clear even if the language is artificial. Good teachers will still have expectations over and beyond the outcomes. I always wanted my students to enjoy mathematics, to appreciate the elegance of a particularly nice proof, and feel that sense of satisfaction that comes from solving a difficult problem. None of these goals would have got past the curriculum experts.

## On Having a Computer as a Teacher

Use Google to search for "How to Solve a Quadratic Equation." You will find a large number of very good videos on the topic. Serious students studying on their own would find these very useful. These videos do exactly what they were intended to do.

Could a student learn an entire course this way without the aid of a teacher? It can certainly be done. Years ago, we had Correspondence Courses that did this from books and written materials. Later they were renamed as Distance Education Courses, and still later they became Independent Study Options or ISOs for short.

Such courses work best when the student is conscientious and motivated. Students who are less enthusiastic and who tend to procrastinate do not do as well. They need the motivation – and the prodding – that a teacher can provide. I have no statistics to prove it but I suspect that the drop out rate for distance education courses is much higher than for conventional courses.

Even for motivated students, the experience of taking a course is enhanced if they can share their insights with classmates and a teacher. A lively class discussion is of great value.

So, no, I do not think that computer based courses will ever replace schools and teachers. They will have an important place in schools, allowing students a range of options that normal staffing would not permit. But students will still need to take some of their courses – perhaps a majority of them – in classrooms, delivered by a real live teacher with real live classmates. We all thrive on the human touch.

John Barsby

## On Behaviour and Discipline

People in general have differing views on crime and punishment, so it is unlikely that a large group of teachers or school administrators will ever be of one mind when it comes to discipline. Some of our politicians want to be "tough on crime". They are in favour of longer prison sentences and tougher parole boards. Others want to place the emphasis on rehabilitation and not on punishment. Some want a legal system in which a given crime results in a predetermined penalty. Others want to consider the background of the offender and take extenuating circumstances into account. On these issues, the general population is split into two camps with only a few people in the middle.

People of both persuasions become teachers. Those who go into administration, however, are more likely than not to be among the more lenient group. I have heard much staff room grumbling over the years from teachers who feel that a student who has committed some offence or other is let off too lightly.

When I first started teaching, I did not think about these matters much. I may have leaned slightly towards the hard line group. But my years at Gordon Bell, particularly my time with Grade Nine Phase Three, made me a member of the other group. It is harder to be tough on the underprivileged and disadvantaged when you actually know them.

One thing I can say with certitude: When dealing with the offender you must allow him to retain a sense of dignity. If you treat him as if he were some form of low life you have little chance of changing his future behaviour.

Discipline decisions are never easy. Every case has to be considered on its own. My tendency towards leniency lessens when an offender has a strong negative influence on those around him. Then, protecting everybody else becomes an important consideration. John Schaffter, when he was headmaster at SJR, handled one of these situations very well. Without actually expelling the student he persuaded the parents that the best thing they could do for their son was to give him a fresh start somewhere else. He even recommended a specific boarding school that he thought would be perfect for their child. The parents thought he had the best interests of their son in mind – and he did.

## On Examinations

Examinations have been mentioned frequently in this memoir, both the ones I took myself and those written by some of my students.

This is not surprising since examinations were very much a part of my life for many years. My sister, five years ahead of me in school, was involved with external exams – the old departmentals – when I was still quite young. I knew the story of Miss McIntyre coaching my father for the Ontario Entrance exams which he wrote in the 1920s. In my family, passing examinations was a rite of passage, a way of proving oneself worthy, a way of moving up in the world. My father, who never did get to go to high school despite doing very well on the Entrance, was determined that his children would have a good education. Passing exams was the first step.

Students today can only imagine what it felt like to write a full set of final exams where each exam mark was your final mark for the course. Everything that came before – tests, assignments, Christmas exams, Easter exams – was all for practice. None of it was worth a mark. Your teacher's opinion of your work counted for nothing. You had three hours to show the anonymous examiners what you could do. That, and only that, determined your fate.

I imagine that feeling remains in countries that have retained examination boards. Scottish writer J. K. Rowling has captured it in the Harry Potter books when the fifth year students write their Owl Level exams and the Hogwarts teachers – including the horrible Dolores Umbridge – can only look on, helpless to influence the outcome one way or another. The Harry Potter books also capture the excitement of the day, usually about three weeks into the summer break, when exam results arrive in the mail.

In Dominion City, the mail arrived by train around 8:00 in the evening. If exam results were expected, the postmaster would often sort the mail that evening instead of the next morning, so those who had post office boxes – and that was almost everybody – could get their results that night. I remember groups of students crowding the lobby of the post office, sharing their results and commiserating with those who needed to write August "supps".

For many years I was very much in favour of external exams. I thrived under that system. It allowed me to see where I placed in comparison to the entire province, not just the dozen or so people in my high school class. It allowed me to win several scholarships. One of them, renewable for four years, paid all of my university tuition, with some left over to go towards my room and board.

The Manitoba High School Examination Board conducted their last exams in August of 1970. By that time only Grade Twelves were being examined. The years 1969 and 1970 were transitional years. Schools were asked to issue their own marks, the way they do today. In those two years, students received both board marks and school marks. Universities, for the purpose of admissions, used the board marks for a student's best three subjects. For the other subjects they used either the board mark or the school mark, whichever was higher. From 1971 onwards all marks were issued by the schools. Years later, when provincial exams were reintroduced they were only for mathematics and English and they only counted for 30% of a student's final mark.

My enthusiasm for the old examination system waned as the years passed. Not having that exam at the end of the year allowed us to tweak the curriculum to closer meet the needs and interests of the students we had. The stronger students benefitted enormously when teachers realized that the time they had once spent drilling students over and over again on typical examination questions could be spent instead on additional topics or a more in-depth covering of some of the set topics.

The exams also put some students at a disadvantage. Those who were fortunate enough to be taught by experienced teachers who had coached students through the exams for many years had a much better chance of passing than those who had inexperienced teachers. There were several teachers at Gordon Bell who prided themselves on near 100% pass rates on the mathematics exam. By contrast, there were years in Dominion City when the pass rate in mathematics was less than 50%.[52] The pass rate in French was often lower than that.

The modern day use of term marks based on tests and assignments has removed that strong sense of anxiety that came with a do-or-die final. There is one down side to it, however. The modern student often feels that an assignment is not worth doing unless marks are given for it. Some teachers in some subjects – particularly essay type subjects like English or Social Studies

---

52  Even strong students could be disadvantaged by an inexperienced teacher. In my Grade Twelve year (in a pre-calculator time) mathematical tables were still important. My class was shown an awkward and often inaccurate method for getting the fifth decimal place. We were never shown how to use the antilogarithm tables. Instead, we used the logarithm tables in reverse, which was not a bad idea but which resulted in answers where that final decimal place could be quite different from what the examiners were expecting. We would all have had several more marks on the exam if we had had one of the experienced Gordon Bell teachers showing us how to read the tables.

– started to give marks for every assignment. We math teachers, assigning homework just for practice, often discovered students ignored our assignments, concentrating instead on those that were worth marks.

I once told some students that, when I was their age, none of our assignments were worth marks. They could not understand this. "Who would bother doing them?" they said. "Or, if you were forced to do them, who would put in their best effort?" Strangely, that way of thinking never occurred to us. We realized that all of this work was important practice for the big examination around the corner.

At Gordon Bell, I had the experience of teaching without any exams at all. The principal was adamant that exams, marks, percentage grades, and letter grades were all a relic of an evil past. "Examinations," he told us over and over again, "are artificial learning barriers." The ideal school would not even have tests. But, since we had to provide parents and universities with some indication of a student's progress, he grudgingly allowed us to have unit tests.[53] He also would have liked to have just Pass or Fail as the final mark but parents wanted more than that, so we ended up with a three-point scale: Superior, Satisfactory, and Fail.

For many of the students this was a terrible system. Once a unit test was over, they did not see that material again and promptly forgot it. There was never a reason to review. It was like walking through the woods looking at individual trees but not seeing the forest as a whole. In Grade Nine they learned to simplify radicals but a year later, when they needed that skill, it had to be taught

---

53 "When you make a test," he once told me, "the marks for the questions should add up to a number like 23 or 37 but never numbers like 20 or 25. That encourages student to stop thinking in terms of percentage marks." This comment was made before calculators were readily available.

all over again. By the time I left Gordon Bell, I was beginning to find ways of subverting this system. In several courses I would add one more unit called something like Overview or General Course Review with a unit test that was cumulative. I got away with it, probably because the principal who was so opposed to examinations had retired by then.

I sometimes wonder if my original fondness for the old departmental exams morphed into my enthusiasm for entering students into mathematics contests. In both, the students are totally anonymous, pitting their wits against an external examining body, and evaluated entirely on what they can accomplish in the time allowed.

At SJR we had a system I came to think of as ideal. There were tests and assignments throughout the year. There was a full set of school examinations in December and another in June. (In my early years at SJR there was also a full set of examinations in March but that was later dropped.) Each department decided on their own how to calculate the final mark. A typical formula might be 50% for tests and assignments, 20% for the December exam and 30% for the June exam. I would sometimes calculate marks two ways – 50-20-30 and 25-25-50 – and give each student the mark that was the higher of the two. In the advanced class, I would even go with 0-0-100 if their final exam was higher than their earlier marks.[54] I always liked to make the tortoise more competitive with

---

54 It should be noted that in the advanced class, I was able to make these decisions myself. In regular classes, where there were two or three different sections, the teachers would decide these weightings among themselves and all do the same thing. At the beginning of the year we would tell students what the various components of the course were worth but there was a caveat. "We might change our mind about this," I would say. "But any changes we make will be to raise, not lower, your mark." I have heard of schools where these weightings are decided by the administration, and automatically

the hare. One would get off to a faster start but if they both ended up as equals at the finish line, I liked to give them the same mark.

## On the Semester System

In a traditional full-year school, students start all their courses in September and finish in June. In the semestered schools, they start half their courses in September and finish them in early February. Then they start the rest of their courses and finish in June.

It is very presumptuous of me to write on this topic. Let me say up front that I have never taught in a semestered school. That concept came to Manitoba in the early 1970s. Gordon Bell did not adopt it until years after I left. SJR never did adopt it. Today, most high schools are on the semester system. The exceptions are mostly independent schools.

Since semestered schools have been around for over forty years at this point, probably a majority of high school teachers today came through semestered schools themselves and consider it the normal way of delivering education.

There were at least two powerful reasons why schools switched to the semester system. It made timetabling immensely easier. When students were taking seven courses at a time, and teachers teaching almost that many, making a conflict free timetable was a herculean task. The other reason had to do with student retention. At risk students – those in danger of dropping out – found it easier to commit to five months of school rather than ten. If they disappeared in February, at least they had completed some credits that they could use if and when they returned.

---

done by a computer. I would have disliked that very much. These decisions are best left to each department.

The traditional school day usually had eight periods of roughly forty minutes each, giving each course more than the recommended 110 contact hours in a year. Semestered schools started out with four periods of eighty minutes, so the contact time was the same. It didn't take long, however, to discover that it is difficult to keep students engaged for such a long period of time. Today many semestered schools have a five period day with classes of about sixty-five minutes. The contact time is less but it does allow motivated students to take extra credits. That is particularly helpful for schools that offer advanced programs like A.P. courses or International Baccalaureate. If students take mathematics every semester, for example, they can complete Grade Nine, Ten, Eleven and Twelve courses in two academic years instead of four. That leaves ample time to prepare for the A.P. or I.B. examinations.

Despite these very valid advantages that semestering offers, I still prefer the traditional school year. Even if the contact time were the same (and it usually isn't) more can be covered in ten months than in five. Students need time to absorb new ideas. It is revealing to observe that the Grade Twelve mathematics curriculum had to be altered when semestering became wide spread. In the years between 1969 and 1973, the curriculum was a very strong one, much stronger than the one I had taken in the early 1960s. But semestered schools couldn't get through it all, so in 1974 it was revised, making the combinatorics unit optional. Most schools dropped that unit, although at SJR, not being semestered, we continued to teach it.

Another concern I have about the semester system is the long gap that can occur between mathematics courses. The same concern would apply to French or any cumulative subject. A student might take Grade Eleven math in first semester one year but not take Grade Twelve math until second semester a year later. That leaves a full year without any mathematics at all, ample time to lose skills and forget many things. The problem might even be worse with French where unused vocabulary would disappear quite rapidly. Compare this to the training of musicians or athletes. If they were to train intensively for five months, take a year off, and then train again for another five months they would not reach the level of excellence attained by those who trained for ten consecutive months.

Sometimes I feel that the semester system is more geared towards the accumulation of credits than it is toward providing a good education. But I have no right to say that. I have never been there. In an attempt to be fair, I started this section with some very real advantages that semestering has to offer. The semester system has survived for almost half a century, so it must have much to recommend it.

## On the Open Area Classroom

From time to time Manitoba schools close down for a day while the teachers attend in-service sessions. In the fall of 1967, my first ever in-service session was held in the city of Thompson which was 160 miles away from Snow Lake School. The entire Snow Lake staff car pooled. The main presentation was given by the principal of the Thompson high school. Her topic was The Open Area Classroom.

This was the first I had heard of this idea but she assured us that it was the way education would be delivered for many years to come. A large open space with four or five teachers and a hundred or more students offered flexibility that the traditional closed classroom did not have. She spoke with great enthusiasm. In the months that followed I heard about this concept many times. Suddenly all the new schools that were being built had open areas and, where possible, some traditional schools were being retrofitted.

## Fifty Years in the Classroom and What I Learned There

When I went to Gordon Bell in 1970, I learned that a new wing had recently been built with large open area spaces for English and Social Studies and a new library. The old library had been converted into an open area space for mathematics. They also had created large open area labs for physics and chemistry. But most of the instructional space was still in the form of traditional classrooms.

So, much sooner than I expected, I found myself teaching in an open area classroom. Some classes I taught met only in the open area, some only in traditional classrooms and some wherever there was space, which was the open area on some days and a traditional classroom on others.

Perhaps we simply did not know how to use the space but I never did see its advantages. In my first year there, the principal wanted all students to work at their own pace through the courses. It was called Continuous Progress. When he talked about it you could hear the capital letters. He envisioned students from Phase One, Phase Two and Phase Three all working together in an open area classroom with each student progressing at his own pace, working from course outlines which were called contracts. There would be at least three teachers in the room, providing students with one-on-one help as needed. Continuous Progress worked very well with the Phase One students, not as well with Phase Two, and was a disaster with Phase Three.

At the end of the year, when hundreds of students had failed to complete their courses, and some were not even at the half way point, the principal relented. In an attempt to repair the damage, he declared that all students would move on to the next course in September, whether they had completed the previous year or not. After that failed experiment, we started delivering many courses in a more traditional manner. But, for me, it had been a very useful experience. In later years, when I allowed some very strong SJR students to work ahead on their own, I knew how successful that can be for the highly motivated. I also knew how disastrous it could be for the less motivated.

With younger students in the open area, we tended to keep our classes separate, each occupying a corner of the room and trying to ignore all the others. With the Grade Elevens and Twelves, after we had abandoned Continuous Progress in Phases Two and Three, we would put the Phase Two classes in the open area, leaving the traditional classrooms for Phases One and Three. In the open area, one teacher would deliver a lesson to the large group. After the lesson, when the students were doing seatwork, the teachers were there to offer help as needed. The material was well covered but the usual teacher-student relationship was different. At the end of the year I knew all the students with outgoing personalities but the more timid or shy students in the group were lost in the crowd.

I recently attended a reunion at Gordon Bell. I found that walls had gone up in the math open area dividing it into four traditional classrooms. The same fate happened to the English open area. The social studies open area had been made into a theatre. Similar fates have happened to open areas in schools all over the country.

The concept did not totally disappear. A new wing recently built at SJR features two classrooms with a folding wall between them. That seems to offer the best of both worlds. Even more impressive to me is the fact that the new wing offers a large number of small seminar rooms, where a few students can leave the classroom to work together on one project or another. That offers much more flexibility than the open area classrooms of the late 1960s and the 1970s. I wish those seminar rooms had existed during my teaching days!

## On Changes in Curriculum

There were many changes in curriculum during the years I spent in the classroom and more in the years since then. Some of these changes are made to modernize and update the course content. Others reflect new theories in education. Others come from the perpetual tug of war between those who want to strengthen the courses, to make our students more competitive with their international counterparts, and those who feel that the present curriculum is already too heavy to deliver in the time allowed.

The need to modernize the curriculum from time to time is obvious. In my high school days, there was very little 20$^{th}$ century literature studied in our English courses. Canadian history ended around 1945. In mathematics, we spent a lot of time learning how to use tables of logarithms to perform complex arithmetic calculations, a skill that nobody has used since the electronic calculator became a household item in the 1970s.

Curriculum changes that reflect new theories in education are more problematic. New theories in education are not like new theories in, say, medicine that can be scientifically tested and proved to be effective. There are too many variables. A group of teachers is instructed on a new way of doing something. They are enthusiastic about it and try it out on their classes. The classes respond to their enthusiasm and do very well. Suddenly this becomes the recommended way of doing things. A year or two later, it is obvious that while it works well in some classrooms with some teachers, it does not work as well in others.

Consider, for example, the reading wars of the last century: whole language vs. phonics. The experts who took a strong position on one side or the other were like political ideologues of the left and right, neither able to see the merits of the other side. In mathematics, the disagreement between those who favour the discovery approach and those who wish to emphasize skills has been equally divisive. Some years ago, I wrote a letter to the editor of the *Winnipeg Free Press* dealing with this topic. The complete text of that letter appears at the end of this section.

It is not my intention to be critical of new ideas and new methods. It is these that have made the schools of today ever so much better than those of fifty years ago. It is my intention to emphasize the fact that teaching methods and curriculum are different things. They are often blurred today.

Textbooks in particular are not merely concerned with content. They are often written in such a way that teachers are forced into using methods that do not come naturally to them. A teacher who wants her students to learn their multiplication tables may have a class set of textbooks written by a committee[55] which disapproves of memorization. In many mathematics classrooms – perhaps even a majority – teachers frequently make their own worksheets because their methods and the textbook methods are in conflict.

Administrators sitting in a class to evaluate a teacher often want to see if her teaching methods conform to the "best practices" currently in vogue, rather than determining if they are effective in teaching the curriculum. Within reason, teachers should have more freedom to use the methods that work best for them.

The perpetual tug of war between those who want the courses to be more rigorous and those who feel they are already too demanding has resulted in the pendulum swinging from one extreme to another as the years go by. I will use Manitoba Grade Twelve mathematics as my example. In the 1920s and 1930s there were separate courses in Algebra, Trigonometry and Analytic Geometry, each with its own exam, and each quite heavy in content. By 1950 the three courses had been merged into one.

---

55 When I started my teaching career, most textbooks had one or two authors. Today they tend to be written by large committees.

Much of the content had been dropped[56] and the course was a pale shadow of what had been in the three separate courses. Course revisions in the late 1960s and early 1970s restored some of the lost content but in the mid 1970s a lot of it was removed once again because the newly semestered schools could not cover it all. In the 1990s, when I was on the Western Protocol curriculum committee, our mandate was to strengthen the course, to make our schools more competitive internationally. A dozen years later a lot of material was removed to make the courses easier to deliver. Today we hear about Manitoba students doing poorly in mathematics when compared to other provinces. The pendulum will swing again. Expect the next curriculum revision to make the course more demanding.

The most dramatic changes to Manitoba's curriculum happened in the mid 1960s through to the early 1970s. They were dramatic for two reasons.

First: The 1957 launch of Sputnik started the space race between the United States and the USSR. Science and math courses needed to be much stronger than they had been. This was the beginning of PSSC Physics, CHEMStudy Chemistry and, of course, The New

---

56   Three content areas that are interesting to look at are combinatorics, trigonometry, and conic sections. **Combinatorics** was studied extensively well into the 1940s, gone completely by the 1950s, back again in the revisions of 1968, made optional in the mid 1970s, and back again in the 1990s. In the recent revisions it was limited to just enough to support the binomial theorem. **Trigonometry** was studied deeply when it was a course by itself. The classic British textbook by Hall and Knight was used. When the three Grade Twelve math courses were merged into one, all but the most basic parts of trigonometry were dropped. Some of it was restored in 1968 and more was restored around 1974. It has survived rather well since then. **Conic sections** were slowly eroded with each successive curriculum revision, and dropped completely in the latest revisions. Even the equation for the circle has disappeared.

Math. It took a few years for these courses to reach Canada but they were here by about 1964. The New Math had a strong emphasis on set theory. It approached algebra by essentially teaching the students the field axioms – words like commutative, associative and distributive were used to explain algebraic simplifications. Elementary school students learned to do arithmetic in bases other than base ten. This was supposed to help them understand place value. Most of this fell by the wayside as the years went on.[57]

Secondly: Until the 1960s the curriculum was a one course fits all program. If you could not handle it, you dropped out of school. That worked well through the 1940s but, when more students started staying in school longer, the courses had to be watered down. But in 1963, starting with Grade Ten, the General Course was introduced, giving students a less demanding alternative. That alternative meant that weaker students no longer had to be accommodated in the University Entrance stream, so it was possible to strengthen these courses.

For science and math courses this was easily done since these changes came at the same time as the post-Sputnik courses were being developed in the United States. But all the other courses were strengthened as well. When I took Grade Twelve English in 1962-63 we studied two novels, Hamlet, three modern plays, assorted short prose and assorted poetry. The examination was entirely on literature. (A separate examination with an emphasis on writing skills had been dropped the year before.) By the time I taught the course in 1967-8 students were required to study four novels, Hamlet, two modern plays, assorted short prose, assorted

---

[57] In 1969-70, when I was a graduate student at the University of Mathematics, one of the professors was quite scathing about the New Math. "New Math," she said "is where students learn that 2 + 5 and 5 + 2 are equal because of the commutative property, but have no idea that either one is equal to 7."

poetry, and to work their way through a textbook that dealt with prose analysis. Fifty percent of their exam was on the literature they studied and the rest was on the analysis of sight passages, both prose and poetry.

When the General Course was first introduced, students committed to either the General Course or the University Entrance Course. Starting in the fall of 1968, students could mix and match, taking the General Course in some subjects and University Entrance in others. Soon the courses were simply known by course numbers: 100, 200, and 300 level courses were the University Entrance courses for Grade Ten, Eleven and Twelve, with 101, 201, and 301 the General Course equivalents. In recent years there has been a return to one course fits all. The new course numbers (with Grade Nine now an official high school grade) are 10S, 20S, 30S, and 40S. Mathematics has got around this by having three separate courses: Pre-Calculus, Applied Mathematics, and Essential Mathematics. They carry the same course numbers. We pretend that they are equally rigorous. I am not sure how it works out with other subjects. I suspect that a common curriculum in, say, history can be taught at many different levels. Schools can pretend that all students have been given the same course.

I will close this section with a few words on curriculum compliance. In the days when the examinations were set by the province, compliance was nearly perfect. By the time I was teaching at Gordon Bell, teachers felt free to modify the curriculum to meet the needs and interests of their students. The principal at Gordon Bell frequently told us to consider the provincial curriculum guides as suggestions only. Gordon Bell was not the only school doing this. In those years – the early 1970s – I heard stories from university professors of students who had never studied trigonometry arriving at university with credit in Math 300. In 1988 the Progressive Conservatives came into power, and their minister of education put a stronger emphasis on compliance. A few province wide exams were introduced, most notably Grade Twelve Math and English exams worth 30%. In the 1997-98 school year the examination results, on a school by school basis, were made public.[58] That lasted only one year. The PCs were defeated in October of 1998, and the new government chose not to release that information.

When I went to SJR in 1975 many of the teachers totally ignored the curriculum guides but in a very good way. The courses they offered were geared for students who were going to university and were for the most part more rigorous and more demanding than the provincial courses. This changed later on. When independent schools started receiving some government money, they agreed to cover the provincial curriculum. That did not stop us from enriching our courses, as long as we included all the material in the provincial outlines. In a few cases we got permission to create our own course, designated as a School Initiated Course (known as a SIC). The curriculum for a SIC had to be submitted to the Department of Education and approved.

My 2011 letter to the editor of the *Winnipeg Free Press*:

> Your newspaper has recently carried a number of articles and letters discussing the teaching of

---

58 These results were released in a booklet. I spent a long time studying the results of the mathematics exam. Without knowing what was happening in the schools, the information could be very misleading. A school might have extraordinarily good results at the end of one semester but not the other. It all depended on when their IB students were writing the exam. One rural school had amazingly good results in pre-calculus. But a closer inspection showed that they had encouraged most of their Grade Twelves to do the applied course, allowing only the very best into pre-calculus. If the releasing of results had continued, and schools were being judged by these statistics, I suspect that more and more students would have been steered away from pre-calculus.

mathematics. I spent many years teaching math (from Grade 8 to first-year university), and I am always amused and slightly irritated at the polarization of opinion between those who want to "go back to the basics" and those who use denigrating terms such as "drill and kill." I always agree with both sides. As a math teacher, I was greedy for my students — I wanted it all.

I wanted them to have a deep and thorough understanding of what they were learning. I wanted them to see how various concepts tied together. I wanted them to have great quantities of important facts and information at their fingertips. I wanted them to be fast and efficient with their algebraic and arithmetic skills.

And I especially wanted them to be good at creative problem solving, able to solve challenging problems that were new to them, not just knock-off versions of problems they had solved before.

To be good at solving problems, I wanted my students to have what I sometimes called a "well-stocked mind" — a mental tool kit that gave them a wealth of information to draw on. I also wanted them to be able to concentrate on analysing the problem without getting hung up on more trivial matters — such as how to do the arithmetic or algebra required in the solution. That is where fast and efficient skills were essential.

My advice to teachers of today is this: You do not need to choose between teaching for understanding and teaching for skill proficiency. You can be greedy. You can do both.

# On the Well Stocked Mind

In my school days memorization was important. We were drilled on the multiplication tables. We learned poetry by heart. History exams required the recall of dates and names and facts.

By the time I became a teacher, in the late 1960s, mere memorization was on the way out. The emphasis was more on higher levels of thinking. Multiplication facts can be figured out if the concept is understood. It is more important to analyse a poem than to recite it. In history the emphasis is not so much on what happened as on why it happened. It is not necessary to know facts, the experts told us, if you know where to look them up.

Now, as I advance through my seventies, I am thankful for the things I know. I have had a lifetime of being able to do arithmetic efficiently because I knew the basic facts. The poetry I learned as a youth is still with me. Some of it is more meaningful to me now than it was back then, and I silently recite bits of it to myself as I walk the track at the gym. When I read the newspaper or listen to the news, I am grateful for my rudimentary knowledge of Canadian history – who was who and what happened when.

I have made it clear in this memoir that I consider the schools of today to be vastly superior to those that I attended so many years ago. This is not a nostalgic cry for a return to a rosy past that never existed. Rather, this is a plea that more respect be given to memorization.

The advantages of going through life with a well stocked mind are immense. The higher level thinking skills are of the utmost importance but it is so much easier to think about things if you have some knowledge of the basic facts. This is a call for balance.

## Fifty Years in the Classroom and What I Learned There

The subject I taught for almost forty years was mathematics. It was obvious to me, as it is to all high school math teachers, that students who came from the elementary schools knowing the basic facts of arithmetic had a huge advantage over those who did not. Knowing the multiplication tables was a start. Knowing the decimal equivalent of frequently encountered fractions without having to figure them out every time, recognizing perfect squares up to at least 400, knowing which two digit numbers were prime, recognizing common Pythagorean triples – all these things are a tremendous asset. And, if the student then increases this knowledge year by year, remembering the relationships encountered in algebra, geometry, and trigonometry, he or she is well prepared for the so-called higher levels of thinking. When it comes to solving difficult mathematics problems a well stocked mind makes a big difference. It saves one from getting bogged down in the mere mechanics of arithmetic or algebra, and allows one to concentrate on cracking the problem. The more you know the more tools you bring to the task.

I am reminded of a very talented student I taught a few years before retirement. He was nominated that year to write the Canadian Mathematics Olympiad. One of the final problems on the paper was, to my mind, very difficult. I had no idea how to start. My student solved it in about five lines. When I asked him how he did it, he explained that everything fell into place immediately after he used the A.M. – G.M. inequality for weighted averages. The benefits of a well stocked mind!

The recent provincial examinations in mathematics provide students with a formula sheet which includes very basic formulas as well as some of the more complex trigonometric identities. Many teachers now provide similar sheets on their tests and examinations. The intention was good: a student who would otherwise do well should not be penalized for forgetting some formula. Unfortunately, this has resulted in many students making no attempt to remember any of the relationships they learn. No Grade Twelve student should ever need a formula sheet to calculate the area of a circle.

I am using mathematics to make my point because that is the subject I spent so many years teaching. But it is not hard to see that the same thing can be said of just about any subject. The more you know the easier it is to acquire new knowledge, to integrate it with what you already know and to discover rich and meaningful connections and relationships.

So my advice to the teachers of today is this: Do not abandon memorization in favour of higher level thinking skills. Do both. They go hand in hand.

## On Vision vs Best Practices

If I count principals, vice principals, headmasters, and assistant headmasters, I have worked under many school administrators. These are not positions I ever wanted for myself. It was more fun to be in the classroom and I knew that was where I belonged. I did, however, serve as head of the mathematics department at SJR for many years.

Some of the men and women who held these administrative positions were people of vision. Others were people who believed in best practices. Both could be – and often were – excellent at their job but in different ways.

The visionaries knew within themselves what kind of a school they wanted to run and worked to make that internal vision into a reality. They did not follow what others were doing. Sometimes, in fact, they were moving in a different direction than their counterparts in other schools. In the early 1970s, when many educators were opposed to examinations, the SJR headmaster wrote an essay entitled "Why Examinations are Important" which was sent to all the school parents.

The best practices people looked to see what others were doing – what works and what does not work – and paid careful attention to what the educational experts were recommending.

Both inclinations have advantages and disadvantages.

The best practices adherents play it safe. The innovations that they introduce have been tried elsewhere with some degree of success. Visionaries take greater risks but they can introduce innovations that are fresh and new. Their schools can offer students something that is not found elsewhere.

Best practices adherents are in danger of embracing passing fads. Think the open areas that were later changed back to classrooms. Visionaries may be immune to fads but they might also miss out on really worthwhile innovations that are happening in other schools.

During my years as a teacher, the ratio of visionaries to best practices adherents has changed. Visionaries once predominated. Today, the best practices approach predominates. This might be explained by the training that principals receive. Years ago they had an academic degree and the usual one or two year teacher training course. Today many of them have taken postgraduate courses in education, specializing in administration.

It is worth noting that a practice introduced by a visionary today might become a best practice tomorrow.

The ideal school administration involves a team whose members have complementary strengths. If possible, it should have both visionaries and best practices adherents.

In my days as head of a math department, I must admit to following my vision of the ideal department. I was not looking around to see what other schools were doing.

John Barsby

# On Randomness Efficiency and Potential

Here are three unrelated topics that I often thought about in my teaching years: the randomness of schooling, the efficient use of time and the vastness of unfulfilled potential.

First: the randomness of schooling. Or should I call it the randomness of life? Student A had a brilliant career as a chemist, simply because she was inspired by her Grade Eleven chemistry teacher. Student B became an award winning writer because of encouragement from a particular English teacher. Student C had no interest in his courses and dropped out of school without graduating. Student D would have dropped out of school if it had not been for the music program. Each of these students might have lived very different lives had they had different school experiences. So much depends on chance. Many parents try to get their students into particular schools to improve the odds of a favourable outcome but some element of randomness will always remain.

Second: the efficient use of time. The teacher says: "The lesson is over. Here are some questions to work on. Do what you can in the fifteen minutes before the bell rings. Finish the rest as homework." Student E gets up to sharpen his pencil. On the way back to his desk he exchanges a few words with a friend. He sits down. He rearranges the materials on his desk. He looks around to see if the teacher is watching. He checks his phone (which was supposed to be left in his locker) to see if he has had any texts. He chats briefly with the student beside him. He reads the first question. He looks to see how many questions the student in front of him has done. He looks at the clock. The bell is going to ring in three minutes. There is no point starting now. He slowly packs up his books and watches the clock. The bell rings. That night he complains to his parents about his heavy homework load. Student F, on the other hand, went to work immediately. He finished before the bell rang and had no homework.

It is also possible to be industrious and still be inefficient. It is possible to spend many hours on activities that are of little value. A classmate of mine in a French course I took long ago filled many notebooks writing out complete English translations of all the French literature we studied. It took a lot of time with minimal returns. A very conscientious student of mine had trouble keeping up with her exercises in calculus. When I looked at her work, it was beautifully laid out. She used three or four colours of ink. Her diagrams were meticulously drawn. An exercise which took her classmates twenty minutes to complete would take her an hour.

Thus we see that efficient students do two things: they use the time available and they use it wisely.

It is not only students who differ vastly in their efficiency. It is teachers as well. There are classroom activities that I think of as being "thin". These are activities that take a lot of time, with the amount of actual learning being rather minimal. These are not all bad. For example, a history teacher might ask students to make posters on a historic event of their choice. Each student might spend fifteen minutes learning history and several hours doing art work. In terms of learning history this is thin.[59] But, if it results in a classroom with walls that are interesting and engaging, and students that are enthusiastic, it is worth it. What the teacher needs to do is to seek a balance between activities that are rich and those that are thin. I always saved my thin activities for periods when student engagement would otherwise be at a low ebb – like the last period in the day before a week-end.

---

59   It is only thin if the time used for the activity is time set aside for learning history. If it is an elementary school classroom where the students all are taking both art and history, and much the class time used for it is time set aside for art, then it could be a very rich activity.

Third: the vastness of unfulfilled potential. So many young people with extraordinary talents never fulfill that early potential. Sometimes it is because their interests lie elsewhere. Some extraordinarily brilliant mathematics students come to mind immediately – students who chose careers that made no use of their remarkable abilities. These are people with many talents, and in a single lifetime it is impossible to pursue them all.

Much sadder are the cases where the individuals tried to pursue their talents but to no avail. These are usually artistic talents – musicians, artists, and writers. These are people who often work at jobs that don't really interest them but dream of one day being recognized for their talent.

There is yet another sad type of unfulfilled potential. That is the student who does poorly in school even though he or she is capable of doing so much better. There are many different reasons why this can happen. I should be an authority on this topic having been such a student myself in Grades One to Four but I am not.

I grouped these three ideas together – randomness, efficiency and potential – and saved them for the end of this collection of miscellaneous topics. I did this because my thoughts on them were vague and nebulous. But as I put my thoughts into sentences and paragraphs, I began to realize that these topics are not as diverse as I thought. They can be tied together. At the beginning of this memoir, I wrote about tenacity or stick-with-it-ness. That, I claimed, was the trait that comes closest to guaranteeing a student success in the school system. Tenacity helps us get over the bumps along the way when the teacher randomly assigned to us is not one who inspires us. Tenacity also leads to efficiency. And tenacity is a must for those who wish to fulfill their early potential.

# Chapter XI.
## *How It Used To Be – A Look Into Schools Of The Past*

The past is like a foreign country, they do things differently there.
(from *The Go-Between* by L. P. Hartley)

Here are a few totally random glimpses into the past. With one exception, they all apply to the schools of my childhood and even to the schools where I began my teaching career. In the one exception, at the end of this chapter, we travel even further back in time to look at Manitoba schools as they were in 1927.

A few of these random glimpses may apply exclusively to Manitoba but most of them apply in one way or another to Canadian schools in general. These are for historic interest only. I am not recommending a return to this vanished world.

## On Junior Matriculation

I graduated from high school twice. I have two diplomas to prove it. The first diploma, dated 1962, was granted when I passed the appropriate examinations for Junior Matriculation. That qualified me to enter the University of Manitoba as a first year student. But, instead, I chose to do another year of high school. My second diploma, dated 1963, was for Senior Matriculation. That qualified me to enter the university as a second year student,[60] which I did in September of that year.

Before 1964 many Manitoba students entered university from Grade Eleven, with Junior Matriculation standing. To achieve this, they had to pass English Literature, English Composition, Mathematics, Canadian History, one science, one other language, and one other course. Other combinations of courses could give Grade Eleven standing but these were the ones required for entering university, i.e. for matriculation.

Students from outside Winnipeg tended to take Grade Twelve, instead of going to university for first year, since it was free and they could live at home. Winnipeg students were much more likely to enter university after Grade Eleven. Schools in the Winnipeg School Division did not even offer Grade Twelve courses until 1938.[61]

## On October Graduations

Graduation ceremonies were not just for Grade Twelve graduates. Since many students went on to university from Grade Eleven, most school graduations handed out both Junior and Senior Matriculation diplomas.

---

60   In this memoir when I refer to my time at university, I retroactively apply the new numbering system. When I mention being in "first year," I was actually in what was then called "second year."

61   The first Grade Twelve courses in the Winnipeg School Division were offered at Daniel McIntyre Evening School in the school year 1938-39. The city of Brandon, by contrast, already had Grade Twelve. In 1937-38 there were fifty-five Grade Twelve students in Brandon, and 230 Grade Eleven students. [Report of the Department of Education for the year ending June 30$^{th}$, 1938.]

Graduation festivities were big in those days but not nearly as big as they are today. Everything was usually done in a single evening. Typically, the school would have a graduation dinner, followed by the Exercises which were open to the public and then a dance held in the school. The Exercises featured the presentation of diplomas, a valedictory address, and usually a guest speaker. Often the valedictorian address was delivered by the top student among the Grade Eleven graduates.

But the presentation of diplomas was a big problem. Examination results were not available until the third week of July. A student who failed an examination could try again at the end of August, with the mark available in early September. So how could diplomas be handed out in June?

This dilemma was not solved in a totally satisfactory manner. Some schools, including the high school I attended in Dominion City, held the graduation ceremonies in October when all exam results were in. The problem with that was that sometimes students had gone on to new lives in distant places and were not able to attend their own graduations. Other schools, including the Snow Lake school where I taught, held their graduation ceremonies in June, handing out fake certificates that were later replaced with the real thing. The problem with this was that some students went through the graduation ceremony but never actually graduated.

## On Grade by Grade Credentials

To graduate today, Manitoba students must accumulate a certain number of credits in the years from Grade Nine to Grade Twelve. Some of these are compulsory and some are options. When they have passed all the compulsory courses and have a sufficient number of credits, they graduate.

It was different in my school days and in my first years of teaching. Requirements were specified separately for each grade. The requirements for Junior Matriculation, for example, are discussed above. Not everybody stayed in school until the end of Grade Twelve. Lesser credentials had to be given out along the way.[62] If you were applying for a job, it was important to know if you had successfully completed Grade Ten. Or Grade Eleven. Or Junior Matriculation.[63] You couldn't wait until the end of four years to add it all up because most students weren't there that long.

Today all courses are given equal instructional time. In the days before the credit system each course had a weighting, indicating how much time it was to be given. For example, in Grade Twelve, English had a weighting of 24%, Mathematics 18%, and most of the others around 15%. On the Snow Lake time table, in a thirty-five period week, Grade Twelve had eight periods of English, six of Mathematics, and five each for the other subjects.

## On the Isbister Scholarship

Alexander Kennedy Isbister (1822-1883) was born in Cumberland House, attended St. John's College School[64] in the Red River Settlement, worked for the Hudson's Bay Company and around the age of twenty went to Scotland to attend university. He became a teacher and headmaster in London and the successful author of many textbooks. He never returned to Canada but never forgot his roots. In 1867 he endowed a prize to be won in open competition among the students attending schools in the Red River Settlement.

---

62 It's somewhat like the English system where students can complete their O-levels or, if they stay in school longer, can do A-levels.

63 Grade Eleven standing and Junior Matriculation were not quite the same. Grade Eleven standing required passing examinations in English Literature, English Composition, Mathematics, History and three other courses. To claim Junior Matriculation standing those three other courses had to include a science and a second language. The only second languages offered were French, German, and Latin.

64 St. John's College School and Ravenscourt School merged in 1950 to form SJR.

On his death he left most of his large fortune to the University of Manitoba.

Over the years, the Province of Manitoba continued to award Isbister Scholarships to the top students writing the Junior Matriculation examinations. The province was divided into ten Isbister districts. First, second, and third prizes were given in each of districts 1 to 9. District 10 was the old city of Winnipeg, essentially what is today the Winnipeg School Division. Because of its greater size this district received three first prizes, three seconds, and three thirds. By the 1960s these prizes were no longer large. First prize was $155, second was $105 and third was $55. Nonetheless, they carried a lot of prestige. Some high schools had plaques on the wall commemorating their winners. I have even seen obituaries which mentioned that the deceased had been an Isbister scholar.

For some years, the province also offered a similar scholarship for Senior Matriculation students. The dollar amounts were similar: $150, $100, and $50. However, it did not carry the Isbister name and did not have the same prestige. That was quite reasonable, since it was assumed that many of the best and brightest of that cohort were already in university.

In 1964, when Grade Eleven was no longer a university entrance point, the Isbister Scholarship was made into a Grade Twelve scholarship and continued as such until 1970, which was the last year the Manitoba High School Examination board operated. Without the examinations it was felt that there was no objective way of comparing students from different schools. The scholarship, which had been around for a century, was discontinued.

The University of Manitoba still gives out undergraduate scholarships that have the Isbister name. Alexander Isbister's considerable endowment to the University was lost to embezzlement early in the last century, so the University has had to find other sources of funds to carry on this tradition.

## John Barsby

My sister wrote her Junior Matriculation exams in 1957 and won the first place Isbister for our district. At that time, students who wanted to be considered for the Isbister had to put a blue seal rather than a white seal on their examination booklets. The idea was that the papers would be marked to a more rigorous standard. The only evidence of this in her marks was that half marks were not rounded up. If I recall correctly, she had something like 77½ in English composition – which, among all the exams she wrote, was the one where the marking is the most subjective!

My turn came five years later. The blue seal idea had been abandoned by then, so I used a white seal along with everybody else. I did not win. It was English composition that did me in, which was strange since that was a subject in which I usually did very well.[65] My other marks were all over 80 – including 83 in English literature, which was quite high for those days. But there in black and white on my transcript was 57 in composition! Gabe Girard, the principal – and my composition teacher – insisted that I appeal it. So I paid my $4 and filled out the form. Whoever remarked the paper changed it to 64, so I did get my $4 refunded but was still out of the running for the Isbister. It was small consolation the next year to win the less prestigious Senior Matriculation scholarship.

---

65  There was a choice of about five essay topics. The one I selected was "The advantages (or disadvantages) of a large school." I chose to write on the disadvantages. This was at a time when small schools everywhere were closing and larger regional schools were being built. I have often wondered if my low mark had anything to do with my contrarian position. Spelling might also have been a factor. When he heard about my mark, our local school inspector, Donald Thom, visited the marking centre and asked to see my paper. The only red mark on it, he said, circled a misspelled word. I had spelled *acquaintance* without the c.

## On School Inspectors

Both in Tantallon and in Dominion City the school inspector would come around two or three times a year. It was his responsibility to evaluate the teachers and to see that all the government rules and regulations were followed. He would spend the day watching classes in session. Sometimes he would go up and down the aisles looking at notebooks. In Grade Ten, I remember him giving us each a sheet of foolscap[66] and asking us to write a paragraph explaining how the electric doorbell worked. That was a popular Grade Ten examination question of the era, and, I suppose, he wanted to see if our teacher had covered it.

Teachers were often rather anxious about these visits. In my Tantallon years our inspector was a Mr. Moir. My memory of Mr. Moir is an amusing one. Our Grade Three teacher wanted us to all stand up and say "Good morning, Mr. Moir," as he entered the classroom. We practised. She would pretend to be Mr. Moir and we would go through the routine. Unfortunately, Mr. Moir had car trouble and did not arrive until the afternoon. Undaunted, we all stood up and in one voice said, "Good morning, Mr. Moir."

In Dominion City, our inspector was Donald Thom who lived in town. He was my Sunday School teacher at one time, so I knew him well. He wrote some letters of reference for me when I applied for scholarships. He also made it possible for me to teach in Dominion City for those two months in the spring of 1965. His children were older than I was but I knew both of them. His daughter, who died very young, directed a high school play in which I was a child actor in my Grade Seven year. His son was in

---

66  Lined foolscap paper – usually pronounced fullscap – was, and still is, widely used for tests and examinations. The unusual spelling has puzzled many students. It is historic. The early manufacturer of this type of paper used a Fool's Cap as his logo and had a Fool's Cap watermark on each sheet.

Grade Eleven when I was in Grade Nine. If I remember correctly, we were both in the tumbling club.

In my first year teaching in Snow Lake, the inspector came around once. There were very few inspectors left by that time. When school districts amalgamated to form divisions, the superintendents assumed most of the responsibilities that had once belonged to the inspectors. But Snow Lake was not in a division[67], so we had an inspector, a Mr. Hjalmarson from Thompson. He watched me teach a science class to a group of students in the Grade Eleven general course. His comments afterwards were very kind. There was no written report. It seemed to me there should have been but one never appeared.

## On Lunch Hour

In both Tantallon and Dominion City, some students lived in town. Others, from farms in the area, were picked up in the morning not by buses but by "vans". The van drivers, who were usually local farmers, could use any vehicle they wanted as long as it would accommodate the number of students on their route. They were paid, not with money but with a reduction on their property taxes.

In the basement of the Dominion City school, there was a dusty box full of foot warmers that had years ago been used in wintertime when the vans were unheated wagons pulled by horses. These foot warmers were metal boxes, covered in woolly sheepskin, with space inside for a hot brick.

It was understood that students who lived in town would go home for lunch. In Dominion City, one elementary school classroom and one high school classroom were designated as lunch rooms for those who lived on van routes. The lunch break

---

[67] In Snow Lake, as in some other remote locations, there was no school board. Instead there was an official trustee who was appointed by the province.

was usually an hour and a half. But in the winter, when days were short, the lunch break was shortened to one hour. The half hour saved from the lunch break meant that the school day ended at 3:30 instead of 4:00. This allowed students on long van routes to get home before dark.

In my Grade Eleven year, the principal, Gabe Girard, decided to make lunch break only an hour long for the whole year. One of the mothers did not approve. Her family had their big meal at noon and her daughters, she said, needed that extra time to wash the dishes. On the first two days the daughters arrived late for afternoon classes. The mother said it would be like that for the rest of the year. On the third day there was a knock on the family's door towards the end of the one hour lunch break. Two high school girls presented themselves. "We're here to do the dishes," they said. "Mr. Girard has drawn up a roster so that you will have two people each day to wash the dishes. Your daughters will only miss classes when it's their turn." From then on the mother did her own dishes and everyone made it to school on time.[68]

In Snow Lake all the students went home for lunch. The school was locked as soon as they left and did not open for an hour and a half. There must have been some working mothers in town. It never occurred to me to wonder what arrangements they made. Some of my colleagues, including the principal, ate their lunch in the school staffroom. It must have been a very quiet and restful place with no students in the building. I wouldn't know. I went home for lunch.

---

68 Human memory is a fallible thing. I have told this story many times but when I came to write it down, I wondered if I had embellished it. Had Gabe Girard merely threatened to draw up that roster? So I asked someone who would know – a niece of the difficult mother. The story was indeed as I remembered it. It was even funnier when the niece described her aunt's reaction.

John Barsby

# On the Grade Eight Survey Test

In my student days, the Manitoba departmental examination system was different in each grade. Grades Eleven and Twelve wrote three hour examinations in every subject. These were centrally marked and worth 100% of the final grade. Grade Tens wrote two hour examinations in just five subjects (English Literature, English Composition, Mathematics, Science, and Social Studies), and these were locally marked and worth only 50%. School marks were issued in the other subjects. Grade Nines wrote exams[69] in four subjects (English Language, Mathematics, Science, and Social Studies) which were centrally marked. The math exam was two and a half hours and the others were two hours. Grade Nine marks were sent not to the students but to the school inspector. He also had school marks submitted to him by the principal. On the basis of this information, he would decide whether a student passed the year or had to repeat Grade Nine. In Grades Ten to Twelve students did not have to repeat any subject that they passed but in Grade Nine a student was either promoted to Grade Ten or had to repeat everything.

Grade Eight was different. They wrote only one departmental examination, known as The Survey Test. The subject differed from year to year. It could be any one of four subjects – English Language, Mathematics, Science or Social Studies – but it was usually either English or Math. The subject was not announced ahead of time. Nobody, including the teacher, knew what would be examined until the sealed envelope was signed and opened on the morning of the examination. It was locally marked and the

---

69 These were traditional full solution examinations until sometime in the mid 1960s when all but the English exam became multiple choice tests. They were discontinued in 1968.

student got to choose between keeping the mark or writing the school exam instead.

In June of 1959, my Grade Eight year, the exam was in Science, which was a big surprise since it had been either English or Math for quite a few years. I had a mark of 90%. Mrs. McVicar suggested that I let it stand and I went along with that. I think I liked the idea of having my first departmental actually count! I clearly was not overly obsessed with high marks, because I likely could have done as well or better on the school exam.

What was the purpose of the survey test? Was it to see how well the Grade Eights in the province were doing? Or, was it a way of enforcing the curriculum – to make sure that teachers did not stray from the prescribed material? Perhaps it was both. Perhaps it was a relic of a long distant past when Manitoba Grade Eights, like those in Ontario, wrote High School Entrance exams.

## On Buying Your Own Textbooks

The government of Duff Roblin was elected to office in 1958. The first of their many changes to education was the introduction of free textbooks, starting in September of 1959. Until then students had to buy their own textbooks. (Some school divisions did provide the readers that were used in the early grades.) At the end of the school year, students received a textbook list for the following year. Many businesses, including Eaton's and The Bay, competed for this trade. But the cheapest way of getting books was to know someone who was a grade or two ahead of you and buy their used books. Condition did not seem to matter. Many students used books so worn that they were in pieces. There was always a lot of grumbling among parents if the textbook was changed or went into a new edition. Some families would be left with a book they couldn't sell and others did not have the option of buying used. The Department of Education was very aware of this and did not change books often or frivolously.[70]

My Grade Eight year was the last year that I had to supply my own books. There was a big buy back at the end of that year. On the last day of school, students were allowed to sell their books to the school for use the following year. I remember getting eighty cents for my copy of *Intermediate Mathematics Book 2*. I sold several others as well but I don't remember how much they were worth. We were paid in coin. Mrs. McVicar came into the classroom with a box full of dimes, nickels and quarters. She rejected books that were in pieces but she accepted the rest, even some that had a lot of marks inside.

## On Examination Fees

In my high school years, students in Grades Eleven and Twelve had to pay an examination fee to cover the cost of setting and marking their final exams. They had to apply for the examinations ahead of time and submit a cheque or money order with the application.[71] Grade Eleven examinations were $1.50 each and Grade Twelve exams were $2.50 each. When I was in those grades, Grade Elevens wrote seven exams and Grade Twelves wrote

---

70 Schools had little choice when it came to textbooks. They were expected to use the books authorized by the Department of Education.

71 I still have the sheet of instructions that came with the application form. It had obviously not been revised in many years since it was delightfully old fashioned even for 1963. It stated, among many other useful pieces of information, that ink would be provided by the school board, blotters would be provided by the Department of Education but "candidates shall provide their own pen holders, pen points, pencils and other necessary supplies."

five.[72] The $12.50 examination fee I paid in Grade Twelve was the equivalent of about $100.00 in today's money. Some friends my age do not remember this. One is certain he never paid an examination fee. Possibly, there were wealthier school districts that paid it for their students. It was eliminated a few years later, a move much approved of at the time by one of the editorial writers in the *Winnipeg Free Press*.

## On the School Register

That large beige coloured book with stiff paper wraps was a record of attendance and it was considered to be a legal document, proof that a student was there on that day at that time. In my first summer school course in education, the importance of the register was emphasized. But I already knew that. In Dominion City the registers going back to the beginning of the century were kept in a storage closet. From time to time, they would be called into service. Individuals turning sixty-five and applying for their old age pensions would suddenly discover that their parents had never got around to registering their births and no birth certificate was available. But if there was a school register from early in the century listing their name and birth date, a notarized letter with that information would do instead.[73]

---

72  When my sister was in Grade Twelve, students wrote six exams. There were two examinations in English – one was Drama and Poetry and the other was Composition and Prose. In 1962 these were combined into a single exam, called, appropriately, Combined English. I have some old exam papers from the early 1940s. Back then students wrote four exams in English. The compulsory exams were: Drama, Poetry, Novel, and Composition. There was also an exam called Optional English. That was for female students who were excused from taking some of the math courses that were compulsory for male students.

73  In my Grade Twelve year, in preparation for Parents' Night, the principal and several of the Grade Twelve students temporarily

In Snow Lake the principal took this very seriously and our registers had to be accurate with attendance taken twice a day, once in the morning and once after lunch. Every month there was a form to be filled out and the register had to be checked by the front office.[74]

Schools still take attendance seriously but it is not as meticulous as it was in days past. Attendance at Gordon Bell was a big surprise to me. We did not even have registers. We kept attendance in a notebook or on scraps of paper. At the end of each month we transferred the information to an optical computer card and handed it in to the office. Home room was morning only and we marked the student present for the entire day without knowing whether that would be the case or not. If students had a spare first period, they did not have to come to homeroom. They could sign in at the office, which many students did not bother doing.[75]

---

converted the school library into a museum, displaying many old artefacts that had been around the school for years, some very old textbooks that we borrowed from an elderly alumnus, and the old registers. The registers were very popular with the parents. Some, who had themselves gone to the school, found the names of all their classmates and teachers. Many years later, in 1991, those same registers were on display again at a school reunion. That time I was one of the older adults, fascinated by this glimpse into my school days. I was able to find my Grade Eight marks, which Mrs. McVicar had recorded in the back of the register.

74  The monthly attendance form asked for Average Attendance to two decimal places. For most teachers, this required long division, dividing the total attendance by the class size. But I had a homeroom with exactly 10 students, so I was always the first to finish.

75  Signing in at the office meant filling out a little slip with name and homeroom number. The slip was then put in the teacher's mailbox. One year a mystery student (who was probably marked present anyway) started signing into various homerooms using amusing fictitious names. The American authorities that year were trying to find a fugitive named Patty Hearst. They were certainly unaware that

Sometimes a student would find me in the hallway and say, "I'm here." I would be dashing from one class to another with other things on my mind. If I forgot all about it, the student would remain marked absent. The absolutely accurate attendance of long ago was only possible in a time when students had less freedom to come and go than they have today. Fortunately, in the modern world, I would be surprised if old school registers are ever used as proof of age or for any other legal purpose.

## On Opening Exercises

Until the early 1990s the school day began with O Canada, The Lord's Prayer, and a Bible reading. The government provided a list of Bible readings for the year. It was clearly stated that the teacher was forbidden to comment in any way on what he or she had just read.

In my elementary school days, the teachers followed these instructions faithfully. The school inspectors were expected to enforce these regulations. Donald Thom, the inspector whose region included Dominion City, described it as a delicate matter. He had been called in by principals on several occasions to deal with Jehovah's Witness families that did not want to stand for the national anthem. When I look back on this, I shake my head with disbelief. Why couldn't the principals work out some amicable compromise on their own?

In high school in Dominion City, we started the day with an assembly where we sang O Canada, said the prayer, heard any announcements, and then sang God Save the Queen. After that we went to homeroom where we had the Bible reading and took attendance. In Grades Eleven and Twelve we tended to skip the Bible reading. Mr. Thom never came around that early.

---

she had reported herself present to at least a dozen Gordon Bell homeroom teachers.

In Snow Lake we went straight to homeroom. O Canada and the Lord's Prayer were played over the P.A. system. The teachers were supposed to do the Bible readings in the classroom, which I did for the first month or so. Then, one day, I accidentally read the same passage as I had read the day before. Nobody noticed. At that point I stopped doing the readings.

By the time I reached Gordon Bell it was the 1970s and more and more teachers were ignoring these requirements. I was assigned a Grade Eleven homeroom, which met in an open area classroom along with two other Grade Eleven homerooms. O Canada was played over the P.A. system. We said the prayer only one year out of the five years I spent in that room because one of the teachers that year insisted on it. We never did the Bible readings. We were breaking the law.

These regulations did not apply to independent schools. In my many years at St. John's-Ravenscourt we did not even sing O Canada except on special occasions like Awards Day or Graduation Exercises. That changed shortly after I retired. They are now required to play the national anthem every day. It is played over a P.A. system that did not exist when I was there.

The religious components of the exercises vanished from public schools some years ago. They were challenged in court by a student from rural Manitoba who had been suspended for not standing during the prayer. He won his case and the religious observations were banned in 1992. Today, there are still a few public schools that include these observances in their opening exercises. Today, they are the ones breaking the law. But now, as then, it is a law that few people want to enforce.

There was, apart from the opening exercises, another occasion where religion played an important role in elementary schools. That was the Christmas Concert. In small towns this was a major event, usually held in the community hall and open to the public. It took the form of a variety show but always included traditional

Christmas carols and a pageant with students taking the parts of Mary, Joseph, some shepherds and the three wise men. It ended with a visit from Santa Claus, who handed out bags of nuts and hard candy. Some schools still have Winter Concerts but most are now completely secular.

## On Skipping a Grade

This was once a very common practice, particularly in the one-room country schools with eight grades in a single classroom. A Grade Four student might be doing very well, finishing his work quickly day after day and sitting idly with nothing to do while the teacher was teaching a different grade. A Grade Six student might be clearly the top student in her grade. She might be listening intently while the teacher was teaching a lesson to the Grade Sevens or even the Grade Eights. These students might well find themselves promoted midyear to a higher grade. If the enrolment of the school was small, there could be just one student in Grade Five. If he was doing at all well, it was often easier for the teacher to just include him with the Grade Sixes.

When I went to university in 1963, I had several friends who were a year younger than I was. They had attended one-room schools and had "skipped" a grade.

The two schools I attended as a child – Tantallon and Dominion City – did not believe in skipping grades. Before moving to Tantallon, however, we had lived in Raith, Ontario. In the one-room Raith School, my sister had completed Grades Four and Five in a single year and had been promoted to Grade Six.

We moved to Tantallon that summer and, to her great disappointment, her new school did not believe in accelerating students and made her repeat Grade Five. She particularly resented having to work through exactly the same arithmetic book that she had worked through the year before.

I have some sympathy with the decision to place her in Grade Five. She had started school a year early. If she had gone into Grade Six that year she would have been two years younger than her classmates. But I am appalled that they would make her do the arithmetic exercises all over again. Did they lack the ability or the imagination to find something that she could do instead? I also see no reason why a Grade Five student could not be working through a Grade Six arithmetic book.

Sometimes skipping a grade worked out well but sometimes it did not. Some quite bright students with poor work habits skipped a grade early on and ended up struggling in high school when the work became more demanding. Others did well academically but did not fit in socially in high school.

One student I taught came to us as a ten year old in Grade Eight. He entered university at the age of fifteen. I can only imagine what it was like for him, far from home, living in a university dormitory where everyone else was eighteen or older. Skipping grades was a big gamble.

I am all for keeping most students with their age group but allowing them to work on their own in those subjects that interest them. Give them interesting books to read. If it is mathematics that interests them, give them challenging problems to solve. Let them work ahead. In the higher grades, let them prepare for Advanced Placement exams. Or let them challenge courses at a local university.

I have had students who finished their Grade Twelve mathematics as early as Grade Nine. Along the way they solved hundreds of challenging problems and wrote national and international mathematics contests. They completed a number of university level courses while still in high school. But they spent a full twelve years in school. [76]

## On Duplicating Machines

The schools of today have much better supplies and equipment than those of fifty years ago. Let me illustrate this statement by discussing duplicating machines. I am sure some large city schools had Gestetner or mimeograph machines back in the 1950s but we certainly did not have them in Tantallon when I started school in 1951.

In Tantallon, in those days, each classroom had one or two hectograph[77] pads. A hectograph pad looks like a firm sheet of Jello. It is yellow when brand new but soon becomes a dark blue. It is made chiefly of gelatine and glycerine. They could be bought commercially but they could also be home made.

The teacher would write the original with a special hectograph pencil. She could also use hectograph ink or, if she wanted to type the original, hectograph typewriter ribbons and hectograph carbons were also available. When the original was ready, the surface of the gelatine pad was moistened and the original was carefully applied face down to the surface.

After a minute or so it was peeled off. The ink had seeped into the gelatine. Blank pieces of paper were carefully applied to gelatine one at a time and each, when peeled off, was a copy of the original. A good hectograph could make twenty or thirty such copies – and even more if fainter copies were acceptable.

---

76 A few of them did their skipping at university. They had taken a number of university math courses during their high school years, and, in other subjects, had taken A.P. examinations. This gave them enough advance university credits to do a four year degree in three years.

77 Sometimes spelled hektograph.

When the last copy was made, the hectograph was put aside for a day or two while the ink diffused. It could then be used again. Eventually there was so much ink in the gelatine that it no longer made good copies.

Even if the teacher had two hectograph pads, she was limited in the quantity of copying that she could do. I can remember exam time in Room II of the Tantallon school, with three grades in the same room. One of the grades would get their exams on hectographed sheets. Everyone else would find their exam questions written on the blackboard. Usually, a wall map covered the questions until the students were seated and ready to start.[78]

When we moved to Dominion City in 1955, the school had a spirit duplicator, which everyone called a "ditto machine." This was much more efficient since it could be used many times in a single day. Part way through my Grade Eleven year the school also acquired a Gestetner. Stencils for this machine were quite expensive, so it was used only occasionally. When I started teaching in Snow Lake, we also had both a spirit duplicator and a Gestetner.[79]

In 1970, when I went to Gordon Bell, the school had the latest in school duplicating equipment. There were spirit duplicators and a Gestetner. There was also a thermofax. If you wanted to make only one or two copies of a document, the thermofax would do it. The copies were on a thin flimsy paper which would turn a dark brown

---

[78] This recollection is for Christmas exams and Easter exams. The June exams were often on cheaply printed leaflets, from an external source that made elementary school exams for Saskatchewan teachers. These were called Basic Achievement Tests. Unlike departmentals, they were marked by the teacher. The school could schedule them for any convenient day or not use them at all.

[79] Different stationery was required for the different machines. Gestetner paper was porous to prevent the ink from smearing. Paper for the spirit duplicator was smoother.

if exposed to bright sunlight. For very special jobs, there was also a device we called a Gestetnofax[80]. This would take an original and create from it a Gestner stencil which could then be used to make as many copies as you wished. The thermofax and Gestetnofax were true innovations since they could duplicate printed material, as long it was a loose sheet and not part of a book.

The first photocopiers I ever saw were at the University of Manitoba in or around 1966. It did not occur to me that these were something that schools could one day afford. When I started teaching at SJR in 1975, the duplicating facilities were similar to those at Gordon Bell, including the Gestetnofax. There was also an early photocopy machine in the office but it was for administration only, not for classroom materials. The first photocopier for classroom materials came to SJR in or around 1980. All the older devices were abandoned overnight. A new era in copying had begun.

## On Fountain Pens

In my elementary school years, ball point pens existed but were considered unsuitable for school use. We all used fountain pens. We filled our pens from bottles of ink that we kept in our desks. The main brands of ink were Scrip and Quink. Most of us used blue ink. Blue black was also quite popular. A spilled ink bottle – and the mess it creates – was rare but it did happen occasionally. I was in Grade Six when I first encountered fountain pens that used prefilled ink cartridges. Some of my classmates put away their ink bottles and opted for these. I was not among them.

By the time I reached high school in September of 1959, many of my classmates were using ball point pens. Was this possible because the ban on ball point pens was just for elementary school

---

80  When I tried to Google that word, I found only one reference to it. It seems they were more widely known as electrostencil machines.

or was this ban lifted as the 1950s were ending? I have no way of knowing.

Once again, I was not an early adopter of this new trend. I continued to use a fountain pen throughout high school. In the four years of university that followed I often used a ball point for taking notes but usually used a fountain pen for tests and examinations. Even in my early years of teaching I occasionally used a fountain pen. A fountain pen with red ink was excellent for marking assignments or tests. The red was bright and vibrant. But it has been many years now since I last used a fountain pen.

The sturdy wood and iron desks[81] we had in the Tantallon and Dominion City Schools spoke of an even earlier period in education when even the fountain pen was banned from the classroom. On the far right hand corner of the desk top, there was a hole about two or three inches in diameter. These holes, which were empty in my time, were designed to hold ink wells. Students learned to write using a "straight pen" – essentially a wooden stick with a slot at the bottom to hold a steel nib. The nib, once dipped into the ink well, held enough ink for three or four words and then had to be dipped again.

The nib splayed slightly on the down stroke, making a wider mark than on the up stroke. For a talented practitioner this could result in beautiful handwriting, sometimes referred to as "copperplate". This type of calligraphy cannot be done with a fountain pen and certainly not with a ball point pen. Teachers of the early 20th century who valued that style of handwriting were loath to give up on the straight pen.

---

81 These desks – the kind that were bolted to long wooden runners – were extremely sturdy and lasted for many years. Some of the desks may have been as old as the school. The desks in the Dominion City school had been refurbished in the summer of 1956. The wooden surfaces were sanded down and refinished and the metal parts were painted green.

Today, it is not only copperplate calligraphy that is a thing of the past. Cursive handwriting itself is becoming less and less important and often is not taught at all. Every year for the last forty years I have been on a team that marks Euclid Mathematics Contests in April. A few years ago, I started watching to see how many contestants used cursive handwriting. There are a few, but very few, students who use it. Most use some form of printing.

## On Corporal Punishment

Corporal punishment was once used in many schools. In the schools of my childhood it was known as "the strap". The approved strap in the Dominion City school was a flat strip of rubber, about two inches wide and covered on one side with canvas. Usually, students were strapped on their hands.[82]

Although individual teachers could use it, they were more likely to send the student to the principal's office where the principal would decide on the punishment. I can recall only one occasion of a teacher administered strapping. That was with a substitute teacher, in my Grade Six year. Her classroom was completely out of control. She attempted (unsuccessfully) to restore order by strapping some of the worst offenders. But these were fifteen year old boys who were bigger than she was and who refused to be strapped. It was a rather ugly scene.

On the whole, I have very few recollections of students being strapped. I do remember an occasion in Grade Seven when the principal threatened to use it. Someone had scratched a four letter word on the wall of the cloakroom. The boys (it was assumed that no girl would do this) were called out of the classroom to meet the

---

82  In the British schoolboy stories I read as a child, corporal punishment was called "caning" rather than "strapping". The cane was administered to the student's bottom. I do not know if the cane was ever used in Canadian schools.

principal. He told us that he was conducting an investigation and would be using the strap as soon as he found out who had done it. It was an empty threat. Nothing further happened.

I have no recollection of the strap being used in either Snow Lake or Gordon Bell. Was this because it never happened or because it was not particularly memorable?

Friends of mine – people my own age – have more memories of strapping than I have. I suspect that some schools used it more widely than others. In every account of corporal punishment that I have encountered, either in real life or in fiction, the offending student was always a boy. What, I wonder, was the ultimate punishment for girls who offended?

There is no precise date that marks the elimination of this practice. It was banned by various school boards and later provincial governments at different times, mostly in the 1970s and 1980s.

## On Cloakrooms

In my school days, I did not know what a locker was. It was only when I went to university that I learned about lockers.

In the Tantallon school (built about 1905) and the Dominion City school (built 1916) every classroom had its own cloakroom. A cloakroom was a long narrow room with hooks on both sides where students hung their coats. Students stored books and papers in their desks. On the old desks, which were bolted to long wooden runners, the storage area was a shelf below the desk top. On newer desks, which were not attached to the floor, the storage area was a drawer beneath the seat.[83] Each student was assigned a desk at the beginning of the year, which was theirs for the entire year. Students

---

83  I had the newer style of desks, with the drawer, in Grades Six, Eleven and Twelve. Every other year, my class had the old wood and iron desks bolted to runners.

stayed in the same classroom all day. In high school, it was the teachers who moved from room to room when periods changed.

Athletic lockers? There was no such thing. Neither Dominion City nor Tantallon schools had gymnasiums. There were no phys ed classes on the time table. On warm days in the spring and fall we would sometimes go outside to play baseball. On a few occasions in Grade Eleven we went to the curling rink to play something called broomball. This was done wearing our ordinary school clothes. There were certainly no changing rooms and no showers. Dominion City School did not have running water.

While my classmates and I were hanging our coats in cloakrooms and storing our books in desks, I suspect that students attending large city high schools were using lockers. They probably had phys ed classes as well and might even have had shower rooms. But I knew nothing about those things at the time.

## On Report Cards

The report cards of my elementary school days were purchased from school supply firms. They were small leaflets, usually on manila tag paper. The names of the subjects were printed either down the left hand side or across the top. Beside or below each subject name there was room for the teacher to enter a mark for each reporting period. There was also space for attendance and rank in class.[84] Some report cards also allowed the teacher to give

---

84 In some classes there was strong competition to see who would rank first in class. For three of my elementary school years – Grades Six through Eight – the competition in my class was friendly but fierce. My main competitors were two girls, named Laurel Froom and Darlene Casper. Laurel was usually the winner. It was Penmanship (which we called Writing) and Art that did me in. No effort on my part was ever successful in increasing my marks in those subjects. I remembered that competition years later when I was teaching at SJR. At a department heads' meeting, we discussed whether or not

grades of satisfactory or unsatisfactory on behavioural traits such as "Works well with others" or "Uses time efficiently". There was very limited room for comments. A comment like "Excellent work" would almost fill the space available. The comment space on the final reporting period was usually used to write something like "Promoted to Grade Five."

There was a space for the signature of the "Parent or Guardian." Students brought the card home after each reporting period. On all but the last reporting period the parent signed it and the student had to return it to the school. At the end of the year the student and his parents got to keep it. It was a document showing that the student had completed a certain grade.

My memories of high school report cards are less clear. What counted was the mark transcript we received at the end of the year from the Department of Education. In Grades Nine and Ten there must have been some kind of school report sent home after the Christmas and Easter exams but I have no memory of it.

What I do remember are the Christmas and Easter reports sent home in Grades Eleven and Twelve. The principal, Gabe Girard, prepared what we would now call a spreadsheet. The student names were down the left hand side and the subjects across the top. The marks of every student in every subject were entered. Copies were run off for each student to take home. The parents had to sign their copy and return it.

In today's world, we would consider this a huge invasion of privacy.[85] But, I can see why Gabe Girard did it. It saved his

---

    art and phys ed should be included in a student's average. Remembering my own schools days, I voted against doing that but my vote was outnumbered.

85  Even in those days, I remember being a little surprised at this. But, in the context of the times it was not unusual. When I went to university, midterm exam marks were posted on bulletin boards, often with the names of the students, not just student numbers.

staff the time required to do individual reports. And it certainly allowed the parents to see how their son or daughter was doing compared to everyone else. But those who had very poor marks – and this was an era when failure rates were high – must have found it embarrassing if not humiliating.

## On School Timetables

These days most school time tables are based on a six day cycle. Some even have an eight or twelve day cycle. If a Friday falls on Day 3 and Monday happens to be a holiday, Tuesday becomes Day 4, and no day of the time table is omitted.

Timetables were once much simpler.

In my Dominion City high school days, the timetable used days of the week, rather than the numbered days of a cycle. If Monday was a holiday, we skipped that day and moved on to the timetable for Tuesday. Snow Lake also used a weekly timetable.

I did not encounter a timetable with numbered days until I went to Gordon Bell. All schools in the Winnipeg School Division had synchronized six day cycle timetables so that students taking subjects like Shops or Home Economics, which were not offered in every school, could spend half a day once a cycle at a school other than the one they were attending.

At SJR, I found myself back on the weekly time table but only briefly. In the late 1970s the school moved to a six day cycle and much later to an eight day cycle.

Most elementary schools have timetables which schedule recess twice a day, usually for fifteen minutes. Very few high schools have recess. It was my good fortune to be in two that did. Dominion City and SJR had both morning and afternoon recesses.[86]

---

86   Recess was supposed to be fifteen minutes long. In my Grade Eleven year, Sandra Waddell, a grade twelve student, was in charge of ringing the school bell. She had an accurate watch. When the

## On Latin

For many centuries, learning Latin was an important part of one's education. Compulsory Latin ended in Manitoba schools in the year 1919. It has slowly withered in the years since then but remains on the books as a high school option to this very day.

In 1962, which was my Grade Eleven year, 469 Manitoba students wrote the departmental examination in Grade Eleven Latin and 90.4% of them passed.[87] The high percentage pass rate is not surprising, since weaker students would likely not be taking the course. By contrast, 8,355 Grade Eleven students wrote the mathematics examination that year and 68.3% of them passed.

The school in Dominion City, like most schools in the province, did not offer Latin. But there were schools that did. When I was in university, I knew several students from Flin Flon who had taken Latin as an extra course throughout their high school years. Recently, at the gym, I recently talked to a retired chemistry professor who was a student at a Jesuit run private school in the 1950s and spoke fondly of his four years of Latin.

---

appropriate time came, she slipped out of class and stood in the hallway ringing a hand bell. She was good at the job. Classes always changed exactly as scheduled. But one day Sandra was away and I was appointed as Bell Ringer. During afternoon recess I was outside enjoying the spring day. One of my friends commented that this seemed to be a very long recess. I looked at my watch. It had totally slipped my mind that I was in charge of ringing the bell. We were almost ten minutes into what should have been period seven. I dashed inside, seized the bell, and rang it. Not one of my teachers ever pointed out my carelessness or mentioned the shortened period seven. They were probably enjoying the spring weather as much as I was.

87  From the annual Report of the Department of Education

Gordon Bell did not offer Latin when I was there. When I went to SJR I was surprised to find it was an option for students in Grades Eight to Ten. That lasted until some time in the 1980s.

Today there are very few Manitoba schools, if any, that offer Latin. A former colleague at SJR recently asked the curriculum branch for the prescribed syllabus. While most course outlines get revised at regular intervals, this one was last revised in the 1980s. The revisions were done by Martin Ainley, who was the SJR Latin teacher.

Would I have taken Latin, if I had had the opportunity? I think it would have been an interesting course. But I probably would have taken it only if it were available as an extra.

## On Parsimony

In the summer of 1967, when I was taking my first courses in education, one of these courses was a very interesting school administration course taught by R. E. Vasey, a retired school inspector, whose teaching career began in 1932. He pointed out that the schools of 1967 were much more generously funded than the schools of the past. He used phys ed equipment as his example. "Today," he said, "most schools have closets filled with equipment. But, years ago, many had only a bat and a baseball. If the ball needed stitching, the phys ed program came to a halt."

The rural schools I attended in Tantallon and Dominion City were certainly among the ones that operated on a limited budget. Neither had a closet filled with phys ed equipment, although, if I remember correctly, there may have been a soccer ball as well as the ubiquitous bat and baseball. Neither hired phys ed teachers nor scheduled phys ed classes. It must have been a required course, however, in at least some grades. In my Grade Ten year in Dominion City, we all received a mark of P in Physical Education, even though we never actually took such a course. On one spring day we cancelled the last period and went out to play baseball. Perhaps that counted as phys ed for the year.

Neither school offered Kindergarten. There were no resource teachers, nor any support for underachieving students. There were no guidance counsellors. There were no provisions made for newcomers who did not speak English. They were just placed in one of the lower grades, with the hope that they would pick up English along the way.

Special needs students who could not be accommodated by the school system stayed at home. The 1964 Report of the Department of Education lists the reasons why 452 school age students in Manitoba were not attending school that year. In today's schools many of these – perhaps most – would be in a regular classroom with a teachers' aide.

The 1960s were a turning point. The small rural school districts – many with just one school – were merging to form large school divisions with multiple schools. School board members were less likely to micromanage the affairs of any particular school. These larger divisions hired superintendents who had once been teachers themselves and were not inclined to pinch pennies. The age of parsimony came to an end.

## On the Year 1927

In June of 1969, while I was still in Snow Lake, I got a chance to visit a ghost town. Herb Lake, once a mining town, had been abandoned in 1948 when the gold mine closed down. It was accessible only by taking a boat across Wekusko Lake, a large body of water that was dangerous to cross except in truly fine weather. Several of the teachers, including the principal, were taken across that day by one of our Grade Ten students whose family had once lived in Herb Lake, and whose grandparents were buried there.

The town contained many buildings in various stages of decay. Some of the houses were still partially furnished. It was not easy to move heavy items in and out of the town. In a shed behind one of these houses the floor was littered with the kind of teaching materials that an elementary school teacher would accumulate over the years. The top layer was covered with dirt and some mould. Underneath, I found a treasure that I have kept all these years.

It was a fifty-six page booklet titled: *Programme of Studies for the Schools of Manitoba,* Authorized by the Advisory Board, June 1st, 1927.

It contained the curriculum for all the grades from one to twelve and for Normal School as well. It also contained the requirements that students had to meet in every grade.

Things were quite complicated in 1927. Students in Grade Nine had to decide on which of four programs they wanted to take: The Teachers' Course, The Matriculation Course, The Combined Course, or the Commercial Course.

The Teacher's course allowed you enter Normal School after Grade Eleven. The Matriculation Course allowed you to enter university after Grade Eleven. The Combined Course, which was a little more demanding, prepared you for either Normal School or university. The Commercial Course was only two years long and prepared you to join the workforce, although there were provisions for transferring to one of the other courses after the two years were up.

The Matriculation Course required you to decide what you were going to do when you got to university. If you were going into engineering, you had to take physics in Grade Eleven. If you were going into medicine or law, you had to take Latin each year.

There was an emphasis on "foreign languages" which included French. I don't know how the people of St. Boniface felt about that! Foreign languages were optional in the Teachers' Course but compulsory in the Matriculation Course. If you were taking only one foreign language, it had to be one of French, German, Latin or

Greek. If you decided to take two foreign languages, then Icelandic and Swedish were added to the list of options.

There were two mathematics courses in Grade Eleven: Algebra and Geometry. The curriculum outline for each takes less than one line of print. Here, in full, is the curriculum guide for Grade Eleven Algebra: "Chapters 1- 25 of the text." Elsewhere, in a list of authorized textbooks, we see that the text was "Algebra, Western Canada Series (the Macmillan Co.) Price 75 cents." Most of the Grade Eleven curriculum guides were longer than this! English Literature was the longest, taking a full page. It looks almost like a modern curriculum guide with a detailed list of what is to be studied.

If you were a male student in Grade Eleven, the two math courses were compulsory. If you were female, and in the Teachers' Course, you could replace Geometry with another option.

When writing their final exams, Grade Eleven students had to be good at spelling. "Examiners will mark mistakes in spelling in Literature, Composition and History. Any candidate having five or more errors in any of these papers will be required to take a supplementary examination, the paper to be compiled from a list of words commonly misspelled and to include a continuous paragraph of average difficulty. Candidates will be supplied on application with a list of words from which the paper will be prepared."

Curriculum guides are also given for Grade Twelve. As long as your Grade Twelve courses included at least one foreign language, it was declared equivalent to first year in the Faculty of Arts and Science at the University of Manitoba. Many schools – perhaps most of them – did not offer Grade Twelve and some that did charged their students a tuition fee.

Grade Twelve students were required to complete anywhere from eight to ten courses, depending on whether they were male or female and depending on the number of foreign languages they were taking. The one foreign language program, for example, required a student to take these nine courses: 1. Composition, 2. Rhetoric and Prose Literature, 3. Poetical Literature, 4. History of English Literature, 5. Algebra, 6. Analytic Geometry, 7. Either Physics or Chemistry, 8. Either Latin or French, 9. Either History or Plane Trigonometry or the Science not elected in 7 above.

I find it strange that a student who wanted to take all three of Physics, Chemistry, and Trigonometry could only do so by carrying an extra course. I am also puzzled about the status of German or Greek. They were on the foreign language list up to the end of Grade Eleven but were not available in Grade Twelve. Students who had Junior Matriculation standing with these languages would have had to go directly to university.

If you were not going to university, you could get Grade Twelve standing without any foreign languages. If you were male you did this by taking the four English courses, all three mathematics courses, chemistry, physics, and history. If you were female you were allowed to replace the three math courses with two courses chosen from a list designated as Options for Women. There were four courses to choose from. Two were additional courses in English and the other two were additional courses in French. They were not a light touch. In one of the English courses these non-mathematical women studied passages from Bacon, The Book of Ruth, Addison, Swift, Johnson, Burke, Hazlitt, Chaucer, Spencer, Dyer, Shakespeare (sonnets only), Habington and Milton. The other English course for women covered Ruskin, Carlyle, Arnold, Huxley, and four plays by Shakespeare. It is notable that these special English courses for women did not include a single literary work that was actually written by a woman!

The first twelve pages of the fifty-six page booklet outlined the curriculum for Grades One to Eight. At the end of Grade Eight, there were High School Entrance Exams, similar to the ones in Ontario. "The Entrance Examination" we are told " is based on the whole Elementary School Programme, and to prepare for it the pupils of each grade should be continually reviewing the work of the previous grades."

The elementary school program had a strong emphasis on what they called Morals and Manners. Some of the topics to be covered sound quite modern! Three examples are The Evils of War, The Rights of Animals, and The Conquest of Science over Ignorance and Superstition.

Others, however, sound very dated, such as The Evils of Debt or the one directed at boys telling them that they should be especially courteous when dealing with girls or women. I particularly noticed one in the Grade Eight section entitled The Danger of Mental and Moral Sloth. It sounds very sententious but is it really any different than the talks I used to give on the importance of stick-with-it-ness? It may be similar but my students would not have taken me seriously if I had talked about mental and moral sloth.

That fifty-six page booklet is a fascinating window into the Manitoba Schools of almost a century ago. It also reminds me of the day we visited Herb Lake. In 1969 the forest was already encroaching on the town. More than fifty years have passed since that day. I wonder what, if anything, remains of the town today.

# Chapter XII.
## *The Qualities Of A Good Teacher Circa 1897*

I can never resist a used book sale. In 1971, when I was in my third year of teaching and still taking summer courses in education, I found a real treasure at the Children's Hospital book sale, which is an annual event in Winnipeg. It was a textbook called *School Management*, published in 1897.[88] The author was John Millar, Deputy Minster of Education in Ontario. The book was written for use in teacher training schools – then called Normal Schools. The price I paid for this used book is pencilled inside. It cost me the vast sum of fifteen cents.

I read it from cover to cover. The textbooks for my summer courses were written by authors who seemed reluctant to make any statements that were bold or precise. It was refreshing to find this book from a previous century, by an author who wrote with clarity and charm and who was not at all afraid to call a spade a spade.

---

88  *School Management and the Principals and Practice of Teaching* by John Millar, B.A., published by William Briggs, Toronto, 1897.

John Barsby

I was particularly impressed with Millar's chapter on the qualities of a good teacher. What he had to say in 1897 impressed me when I read it in 1971 and it still impresses me today.

That said, some of the details are specific to the schools of his time. Many of the teachers he was writing for would have taught in rural schools where Grades One to Eight shared the same room. Others would have taught in the graded schools of cities and large towns. High school teachers in his province dealt with a superior group of students, since the Ontario Entrance Examinations, held at the end of Grade Eight, determined whether or not a student was allowed to proceed to high school. The world has changed a lot since then but much of what he has to say is as true today as it was in 1897.

The first quality he mentions is **Good Health.** "A person with a sickly constitution," he says "will break under the mental strain of the schoolroom." He emphasizes the importance of exercise, good food, fresh air, and bathing. "The school," he says, "has no place for the indolent, sleepy, lethargic teacher." If modern readers find this rather sententious, they will really cringe when he flatly says "Other callings should be sought by 'the halt, the lame, and the blind.'" While I find this abrupt dismissal rather disturbing, I recognize there is truth that lies behind what he has to say. It was health considerations that caused me, in my final years of teaching, to switch from full time to half time and in the end to retire before I otherwise might have.

Millar's second quality is **Scholarship.** He wants his teachers to be well educated, to be logical thinkers and to know their material far in advance of what they teach. He boldly says: "High scholarship commands respect but ignorance is despised even by children." If modern textbooks were to say the same thing, it would come out something like this: "Contemporary studies suggest that a certain degree of exposure to advanced academic material is an asset to teachers, even those teaching elementary courses, since students, even the youngest among them, seem intuitively to know whether a teacher's mastery of the content is adequate and will have a tendency to judge him or her harshly if it is not."

In the scholarship section, Millar also tells a wonderful story about Dr. Arnold, headmaster of Rugby, and father of the poet Matthew Arnold. When asked why he spent hours every day preparing lessons on material that he had taught many times before, his answer was, "I wish my boys to drink from a running brook and not from a stagnant pool."

Millar's third quality is **Professional Attainments.** Many schools in his time hired teachers who had no formal teachers' training courses behind them. "No person," Millar says, "should be allowed to teach who has not attended a training school." I have mixed feelings about this. In my student days, there was a severe teacher shortage in Manitoba, and our school had a number of untrained teachers who were in the classroom with a "permit" or "a letter of authority." My own teaching career began before I was fully qualified. Later on I taught at an independent school at a time when many of the teachers there had no formal training. I can assert emphatically that unqualified people can be excellent teachers. On the other hand, in support of Millar, I can also say that the very worst teachers I have ever known were among the unqualified. They would not have obtained a passing grade in a training course – certainly not one with a practice teaching component.

Millar's fourth quality is **Personal Magnetism.** This is much more subtle. "The great teachers of the past had an element in their character which gave them power to influence and control children." They had that personal magnetism "which brings a man friends and surrounds him with associates, though he may have neither wealth nor power to bestow." Perhaps this is what we would today call charisma. While he lists it as a desirable trait, he also recognizes that it comes with some danger, and warns us not to let it blind us to deficiencies in other areas, such as scholarship.

Millar's fifth quality is **Executive Ability**. How true this is – even more today than in Millar's time. When I started teaching, the job was almost entirely in the classroom. Executive tasks involved maintaining the register and writing student reports at the end of term. But as the years passed there was more and more paperwork to be done, meetings to attend, phone calls to be made, emails to be answered, forms to be completed, and deadlines to be met.

Millar's sixth quality is **Tact**. He gives many examples of the tactful teacher. Here are a few quotes:

"[He] does not needlessly irritate or jar the feelings of children."

"An angry parent is met in such a way as to become a friend."

"The people of the entire community regard him with confidence and respect."

His seventh quality is **Common Sense**. "A lack of common sense will cause a teacher to give lessons far too difficult, to put an absurd question to a pupil, to make uncalled-for remarks, to discourage a timid child, to whip a boy for a trifle, to keep the school room uncomfortably warm or cold, and to do many other senseless things where only a little judgement is needed." It is easy to agree with Millar on all of this, although the implied message that it is okay to whip a boy for something really serious shows how the world has changed in the last 125 years.

The eighth quality is **Vigilance**. The teacher must know what is going on in the classroom. Millar suggests that the vigilance should be "that of a kind sympathetic friend rather than that of a lynx-eyed detective." Vigilance, he stresses, prevents discipline problems from arising.

The ninth quality is **Heart Power** which he defined as "the ability to win and retain the confidence and the love of children." I feel this is one of the most important qualities on his list. In Millar's time there were many teachers who relied only on fear to maintain order in their classroom. Think of Mr. Phillips in *Anne of Green Gables*. Such teachers, Millar strongly condemns. He devotes a whole page to Heart Power and uses three historical figures to demonstrate his points: Pestalozzi, Dr. Arnold, and "He who said 'Suffer little children to come unto me.'"

The tenth and second last quality is **Will Power.** The teacher must be able to control himself. "Hasty words, petulance, sudden flashes of anger or chronic sullenness will destroy any teacher's chances of success." But will power does not mean having an iron will. That is "sure to blast all the finer feelings of children and to make them discontented, deceitful and quarrelsome."

The last quality mentioned is **Moral Character**. He is surprisingly brief on this topic and put it in last place! Was that because in late Victorian times it was taken for granted that the teacher would be a pillar of virtue in the community, so it was hardly worth mentioning? Or did he leave it for last place because he was weary of it being mentioned over and over again by other authors and by those who taught teachers?

Most of us who have spent a good part of our lives in schools will have our own ideas about the qualities of a good teacher. Someone I respect very much once told me that only two qualities were needed: you had to know your material and you had to like young people.

If I were making my own list, there would be two things I would stress. The first one is this: Good teachers treat their students with dignity and respect. There is no place for sarcasm or put-downs. If a teacher is genuinely angry with a student it is acceptable to show it but not to say anything that is biting or cruel. The second thing I would stress is this: Teachers should be interested in and passionate about the material they are teaching. Enthusiasm is contagious. If teachers are enthusiastic about their subject, many of their students will also become enthusiasts.

I have not found a modern list of qualities that resonates with me as much as this list from 1897. I find an element of truth in every one of his qualities, though I might not agree with all the details and I certainly recognize that he is a product of his times. We are a kinder and more tolerant people today than we were back then. Despite this tolerance, we tend to judge people from the past harshly for ideas they embraced and attitudes they held. This is a time when we are tearing down statues of people we once venerated. But the people of the past had wisdom as well and it shows clearly in the pages of *School Management*, one of the best finds I ever made at the Children's Hospital book sale.

# Afterword

I am now in my eighteenth year of retirement. My former students are scattered around the country – indeed, around the world. The oldest among them have recently reached the age of seventy and the youngest are now in their mid thirties. From time to time I hear from some of them. Others I read about in the newspaper or see on television. Some I run into in the shopping mall or at the gym. Some are among the doctors and nurses I meet at medical appointments. They all seem to be leading interesting lives, doing things that are useful and valuable. I like to think that the schools where I taught, in some small way, prepared them for that.

I look back on my years of teaching with enormous pleasure. There were good times and bad times. I have not entirely forgotten the bad times, such as trying to teach geometry to that difficult Gordon Bell class that was scheduled to meet in the lunchroom. But memory seems to filter out those experiences. What I mostly recall are the good times. I especially remember the magic that so often unfolded in and out of the classroom. There are many moments – moments of laughter and of joy – that are etched forever in my memory.

I was very lucky in my career. I taught under several outstanding school administrators. I had many wonderful colleagues. And year after year I had many fine students.

I also have very positive memories of my own school days. They now belong to a distant past but in memory they are very much with me. I can see the interior of every classroom. I can remember where I sat. I can see the front cover of almost every textbook. I remember the names of all the teachers. Some of them – I have indicated which ones in this memoir – were very important people in my life.

When I went into teaching in 1967, I was convinced that the work of a teacher was of great importance, that the education of the young was one of the most vital endeavours in any society. I still think that.

Much of this memoir was written during the early days of COVID-19, a time of lockdowns, anxiety and caution. Writing these pages allowed me to time travel, escaping the bleakness all around me and visiting the past.

The past! It lies behind me, infused with a golden glow. Did all of it really happen? Or is it just a dream?

# Acknowledgements

In writing this memoir, I received helpful input from a number of people.

Mark Duncan who taught English at SJR for forty-one years was writing a book called *Seven Meditations on Education*[89] at the same time that I was writing the first draft of this memoir. We each edited what the other was writing. Many drafts later, Mark has gone through it once again. His suggestions have made the text cleaner and tidier – and richer in commas. (But any commas that are still missing are my responsibility!)

Beverley McTavish carefully read through the manuscript looking for typos. Bev, who is now a retired teacher, was a member of that magical Grade Twelve class in Snow Lake, described in the chapter called Magic in the Classroom.

My sister, Pat, and her husband Derek Whitmore, also read through a near to final draft. We spent a long time discussing my Grade Seven reading habits. Derek, like me, had been a childhood fan of Arthur Ransome. Pat and I had read many of the same books. The discussion was reminiscent of a book club – except for the fact it was based on books we had read sixty-five years ago. That led to some revisions in the text.

---

89 *Seven Meditations on Education* by Mark Duncan is available on Amazon.

Other early readers of this work who made helpful suggestions were Steve Johnson, Deryn Lavell, and Ray Grynol. Deryn and Steve were in Bermuda at the time, where Deryn was head of a school that, many years ago, had practised "caning". Discussing this with Steve inspired the short section on Corporal Punishment.

At the age of thirteen, when I shared some of my writing in a very limited way, I used a hectograph pad purchased from D. W. Friesen Co. in Altona, Manitoba. It seems like a strange coincidence that now, sixty-three years later, it is their related company, FriesenPress, that is publishing this work.

The FriesenPress editor who evaluated my manuscript made a number of useful suggestions. As a result, I changed the order of some chapters and made a number of technical changes,

Printed in the USA
CPSIA information can be obtained
at www.ICGtesting.com
LVHW050321310823
756313LV00001B/4